Children of A Certain Age

ADULTS AND THEIR AGING PARENTS

Vivian E. Greenberg

LEXINGTON BOOKS
An Imprint of Macmillan, Inc.
NEW YORK

Maxwell Macmillan Canada
TORONTO

Maxwell Macmillan International
NEW YORK   OXFORD   SINGAPORE   SYDNEY

Library of Congress Cataloging–in–Publication Data

Greenberg, Vivian E.
Children of a certain age : adults and their aging parents / Vivian Greenberg.
p. cm.
ISBN 0–02–912825-0
1. Aging parents—United States—Family relationships 2. Parent and
adult child—United States.   I. Title.
HQ1063.6.G737   1994

306.874—dc20   93-38800
                                                      CIP

Lexington Books
An Imprint of Macmillan, Inc.
866 Third Avenue, New York, N. Y. 10022

Maxwell Macmillan Canada, Inc.
1200 Eglinton Avenue East
Suite 200
Don Mills, Ontario M3C 3N1

Macmillan, Inc. is part of the Maxwell Communication
Group of Companies.

Printed in the United States of America

printing number

1 2 3 4 5 6 7 8 9 10

To my daughter, Jill Rosenthal Hugick, who more than anyone has taught me what being a parent is all about.

Contents

Acknowledgments

Whenever I wonder how this book made it to the finish line, the reason is always the same: Margaret N. Zusky, Senior Editor at Lexington Books. Without Margaret's unflagging encouragment and gentle prodding to look deeper and further, I surely would not have finished my manuscript. Always there for me with honesty, patience, and a sense of humor that made me laugh when I wanted to cry, she was mentor, mother, and muse rolled into one. There is no way I can adequately thank her for her unconditional support.

Thanks also to Margaret, Ann Hall was asked to do the copyediting. With complete respect for my intent and tone, she meticulously applied her red pencil to what needed to be changed. Her editorial touches made a big difference, and I thank her for a job well done.

Special thanks to my dear friend and colleague, Elaine Gross, who took time from a busy schedule that included caring for her 93-year-old mother to read my manuscript from start to finish and to tell me what she thought. Others who contributed with helpful suggestions and relevant source materials were Marsha Albert, Marjorie Bayersdorfer, Barbara Bristow, Jan McCurdy, and Renee Miller. Friends as well as colleagues, they generously gave their emotional support when I needed it most.

To my son, Bob Rosenthal, psychiatrist and writer and his mate, Emmanuelle Rose, savvy student of human nature, my love and appreciation for their boundless graciousness. What good sports they were that week in Sausalito when I relentlessly hounded them for last-minute advice about my copyeditied manuscript. Although they threatened many times to hide the manuscript while I was vacationing with them, they didn't. It's a good thing, because their help was invaluable.

To Biff, Jo, and Margie, dearest friends, my eternal thanks for their good nature and patience. Not once did they become annoyed or angry when I snapped, "I'm sorry, I'm too busy to talk!"

Of course, the many clients, friends, and others who agreed to be interviewed have my unending gratitude. They are truly the flesh and blood of *Children of A Certain Age*. Special thanks, however, to Linda and Fred Hipp, Dot Magee, Joan Rose, and Jane Thomas, who because of their extraordinary openess and trust gave above and beyond.

And to Stan, forever there for me—from getting the printer running to hearing my fears and doubts—all my love.

Introduction

Several years ago, I wrote a book titled *Your Best Is Good Enough: Aging Parents and Your Emotions.*[1] The book was designed to help those middle-aged people commonly referred to as the "sandwich generation people," who are faced with the problem of caring for their elderly parents while at the same time meeting the demands of their own families and jobs. I offered strategies to help these beleaguered caregivers balance their busy lives and also emphasized how important it is for them to nurture their own well-being while being dutiful sons and daughters. The book's main point was that until children learn to honor themselves, they cannot truly honor their elderly parents. In making their need for rest, leisure, and socialization secondary to their parents' needs, they will become resentful, angry, and seriously stressed. They will ultimately burn out and will be no use to themselves or to their elderly parents, who need their support during their later years. The quality and spirit of care given by emotionally depleted people is questionable. What parents want their child to become ill while caring for them? Only the most dysfunctional mother or father, someone akin to Neil Simon's cruelly egocentric Grandma Kurnitz, would want this to happen.[2] As the protagonist of his play, *Lost in Yonkers*, she epitomizes the kind of parent for whom children are merely objects, to be treated without respect for their welfare or feelings. Whether brandishing her cane, stomping her feet, or hurling cruel words, she browbeats her grown children into total compliance.

Yet, many children *are* being stressed to their limits in giving care. And many elderly parents, though hardly as abusive or demeaning as Grandma Kurnitz—in fact quite normal folks—harbor irrational and unrealistic expectations of what their children owe them or can do for them.

Caregiving, a term unheard of 20 years ago, is a complex

process. More than filling a parent's needs for physical survival, it includes a wide range of human forces involving family history, family geometry (the entanglements that define all intimate relationships), individual personalities and coping resources, and the differing lifestyles and values of family members. Throw into this mix the sociological, demographic, and economic factors that affect how we live and relate to one another in today's busy world. As a result, caregiving is worth every bit of the scholarly research and popular attention it now receives. Because of the toll it takes on people's lives, it has become a focal point in medicine, social work, nursing, and psychology. In gerontology it is bound to the quality of life for elderly men and women.

The complexities of caregiving remain the same as when I wrote about them several years ago, and provide an important framework for this book. I have come to recognize the effect of another, stronger force on the caregiving process and the parent-child relationship in general, however. That force, which exists to a significant degree in many parent-child relationships in the later years, is the immaturity and inflexibility of both parties in managing the natural conflicts that characterize this stage. As I counsel and talk to grown children and their elderly parents who are trying to make sense out of their relationship at this time of their lives, I am struck by this resistance, this unwillingness to bend on the part of *both* generations.

I emphasize "both," because when I wrote *Your Best Is Good Enough*, I applied the concept of growing up only to caregiving children. Although I had by then counseled many parents who astounded me with their immaturity, I did not explore it further in that book.

The closest I came to the issue of maturity for *both* generations in *Your Best Is Good Enough* was in referring to a friend who had been living amicably with her mother, then an octogenarian, for 35 years. When I asked her what the secret was to their harmonious relationship, she said, "Tell them, Viv, it takes maturity to make the caregiving experience work. It's as simple as all that, and I really don't see what all the fuss is about." I replied, "It does take maturity. The rub is most of us are not so lucky to have mature parents or to be so fully grown up ourselves."[3]

Now, years later, I am convinced the notion of mature parents and mature children needs to be reexamined. If any kind of positive connection between generations is to happen during their final years together, it will take *two* equally comitted and grown-up parties.

What really put all the pieces together for me in terms of immature parents was an article about Joan and Erik Erikson in the *New York Times* in June, 1988.[4] Perhaps it is because the Eriksons, scholars in the field of human development, are themselves in their 80s. As a result, they are more than just academics looking down from some ivory tower, they are people who are actually living old age. What they had to say made quite an impression on me.

In discussing the final phase of life, which is supposed to culminate in wisdom, the Eriksons told us some folks simply miss the boat. Although wisdom can only truly come with old age, many elderly are unable to do the painful work of reflection and evaluation that spawns it.

Although I had known all this (What professional who works with the elderly doesn't?) it just didn't occur to me that I could use this phenomenon to explain what was happening to the many disappointed parents I was seeing. The idea that wisdom has more to do with examining life's experiences than formal learning finally penetrated when I read these words of Joan Erikson: "You put such a stress on passion when you're young. You learn about the value of tenderness when you grow old. You also learn in late life not to hold, to give without hanging on; to love freely in the sense of wanting nothing in return." If the ability to let go and to love without strings are facets of wisdom, then it is no surprise that so many parents are "ungrown-up."

The fact is, parents, like children, must continue to grow and to learn; to always be open to life's lessons. Often, a parent's most valuable lessons come from some disappointment over what a grown son or daughter has or has not done. Out of the disappointment over a son's lukewarm show of devotion or his decision to follow an unacceptable path, for example, a parent who is willing can find insights and answers leading to growth and inner peace. If parents can't grow up, if they can't turn these disappointments into a kind of wisdom that will guide them in the later years when they need their children's emotional support, they will feel their children have abandoned them.

Although mastering the tasks leading to wise adulthood is harder in later life, it still can be done. Age does not diminish the capacity for growth and change. Letting go of what cannot be, learning to accept and respect those we love as they are, and giving up our illusions of how much of life we can control ought to be easier in later life. Elderly parents have more time to reconsider past choices and actions and to develop different perspectives about what goes into a mutually gratifying relationship with their children.

Still, I am continually astonished by the immaturity of parents who have been my clients and those I know as friends or relatives. They have not done the work of becoming wise adults. Hardly aware that the next important stage in their development is to let go of their children as children and respect them as adults, they cling to their parental role. It doesn't matter that their children are well into their autumn years. They persist in telling their children what to do and how to do it, generally invading their private worlds. Whether they reprimand them for spending too much money on a car or not telling them of their whereabouts on a particular day, or insist they telephone this aunt or invite that uncle to dinner, parents violate their children's adult boundaries. Unaware of the irreparable harm they do to a relationship they both cherish and need, they sincerely feel they are right in their authoritarian role. A parent has certain inalienable rights that last a lifetime, they protest. With this in mind, they believe their children owe them unlimited time, loyalty, and care regardless of their own needs and personal well-being. They push, demand, intimidate, and manipulate on the basis of rules and norms that were relevant when their children were young and dependent. As if caught in some kind of time warp, they continue to see their now-adult offspring as helpless babies requiring their guidance and protection.

The role of a parent shifts with the changing needs of the family over time. The care and comfort required by an 11-year-old child is substantially different from the needs of a child of 25 or for that child when he or she is 50. Parenthood, if it is healthy, is always in a state of change and growth. Never at rest and, consequently, life's least-boring job, it must be constantly revised and reworked in response to the natural changes in the family unit. Ideally, it keeps pace with the needs and sensitivities of children who are different from what they were like in the past. As I explain in Chapter 4, parents who are open and responsive to their children not only grow and learn from them but keep up with the times and feel rejuvenated. Parents who are open to their children, who are able to let go of old roles and ways, and who are able to love them without expecting anything in return are, as Joan Erikson says, wise.

Feeling their children do not care and fearing abandonment, many elderly parents push and pull at them for proof of love and devotion. While their children may not have abandoned them, society, however, certainly has. There is an explicit message to elders in a society where the gifts of youth are prized over the gifts of old age: to be over 50 is to be over the hill. At this point, no one cares about people too old to look good in a swimsuit or in aerobics gear at the local spa. Unfortunately, the elderly often unconditionally buy into these myths and internalize them into their psyches. The result is that even when their well-meaning children demonstrate their devotion, they refuse to believe their children are sincerely committed to their welfare. Given the pervasiveness of youth-oriented propaganda, it is a simple step for parents to project society's shallow and rejecting attitude upon their children. Given this collective negative attitude, no matter how attentive and caring their children, how can parents feel valued and cared for?

Furthermore, at a time when parents experience loss after loss, is it any wonder they cling to the role of parent for a sense of self and power? At least as parent, they have some semblance of control over their world. If their children still listen and obey, somehow parents feel cared for.

Control, however, masquerades for the security of affection and closeness. Underneath the carping about their children not doing enough or the demands for more time and attention is the craving for emotional connection. Says gerontologist Elaine Brody in her book, *Women in the Middle*:

> Emotional support is the most universal form of family caregiving, the one most wanted by older people from their children and the one the adult children themselves feel is the most important service they can give. . . . It is also the kind of help for which no gov-

ernment or paid worker can substitute. Emotional support includes being the confidant, or the one with whom problems can be talked over; providing social contacts such as phoning, visiting, or taking the elderly person to family events; and help with decision making.[5]

At a time then when emotional connection with their children means the most, many parents do not know how to attain it. Although they want to be part of their children's family and especially involved with their grandchildren, they do not quite know how to make it happen. If they only would pay attention, they would clearly see that their old rules for parent-child etiquette no longer apply. Authoritarian statements on what is proper only create distance and hostility in their children's hearts. The affection and intimacy older parents so yearn for can never be achieved through bossiness. Warm connections do not occur when parents insist that they always know best, that children have no right to disagree, that parents come before spouses, and that it is okay for them to address their children without courtesy or respect. Parents need to know healthier ways to get their needs met.

As a 60-year-old daughter of a 90-year-old father, I can attest to my own flashes of immaturity. While my father never pulls rank on me, I have my own moments of feeling very young, indeed. It's just a feeling that unexplainably clicks on at times; an emotion from long ago that renders me small and powerless. Sometimes it's triggered by how he nods his head when I'm writing checks for him, as if he's saying, "Now, you're doing that just fine, dear." Other times it may be nothing he's saying or doing; it's just sitting across from him at the table or next to him in the car, even though I'm in the driver's seat.

Through counseling hundreds of people in my situation, I know I'm not alone. It was especially reassuring to hear perfectly poised Scott Simon, Saturday anchor for the NBC Today Show, announce to millions of viewers that he still worries about whether his mother and her friends approve of the clothes he wears on tv.

We remain children in a psychological sense for a long time. Although we think we have grown up, a certain word or look from a parent can still pierce our adult facades. At times we fear our parents' anger or we have trouble simply disagreeing with them. Other times we feel guilty when we can't always please them.

Ted, a 53-year-old manufacturer of computer software, describes the feeling of powerlessness this way. "It seems whenever I enter my parents' home, I enter a different zone—a twilight zone of childhood where I feel like I'm 12 and have to be a good, dutiful little boy. I'm stripped of my adult confidence and feel very vulnerable to my parents' criticisms."

The same parental superpower that stripped Ted of his confidence, however, can also do the reverse—it can bestow upon children powerful gifts. When used positively by a parent to validate or support, it can cause a grown child to feel infinitely wonderful and capable. Roz, a 57-year-old social worker, describes how she felt after her 83-year-old mother phoned to tell her that she finally understood and approved of what she did:

> I couldn't believe how pleased I was when my mother called from Florida to tell me how proud she was of what I did. For years she has derogated my profession, telling me what I do is worthless because I make little money and have no prestige. It seems she saw a program on television about child abuse, where a social worker was leading groups for abusive parents. Well, after the program, she told all her friends that's what I do. I glowed all over like a high school student bringing home a good report card, because she finally gave me this longed-for recognition.

Or consider the example of Marilyn, 42, whose 70-year-old mother immediately flew 1,500 miles to see her after she broke the news to her mother by telephone that she was ending her 10-year marriage:

> I couldn't have had a better friend than my mother. She not only gave me all her support, but really wanted to hear all about what had happened. She just made me feel so good about myself and seemed to genuinely understand *everything*. And her support meant more to me than my friends'. There's something about getting strokes from parents that can't be duplicated by anyone else. And because she had confidence in me to make it, I knew I would.

Sporadic feelings of being a child are natural and okay. They are vestiges from an earlier era in our development and like embers, they burn for a long time. These feelings are benign and can occur in the most mature people. Moreover, they can even be the source of warm anecdotes that we treasure and that we may share with friends and even our parents themselves.

When these childlike feelings are grounded in fear and interfere with the way children live their lives and feel about themselves, however, they become problems requiring attention. When, grown children who are 50, 60, or 70 years old, successful in their job and greying tremble at the prospect of telling a parent they need a weekend away from caregiving chores, there is a problem. Also troubled is the 51-year-old woman who, eager to spend time alone with her first grandchild, must lie to her mother about where she is going or else give in to her powerful cajoling and intimidation and take her along.

Stories abound in my caregivers' group, for example, about how children are afraid to tell parents that what they spend for veal chops or a winter coat is none of their business. Or they may even hold back from sharing with their parents that despite their objections, they are sending their child to a certain summer camp. In both instances they are unable to let their parents know that interfering in their daily personal decisions is not appreciated. Sometimes, it is something as simple as asking a parent not to phone so frequently. Or it might be a 55-year-old daughter who, afraid of her father's anger, can't tell him she would like to turn on the air conditioner because it's almost 90 degrees in the house. Instead, with tears streaming down her face in frustration and rage, she walks around the block again and again.

Are these mid-life adults, I wonder, supposedly seasoned and secure in their identities, or are they elementary school children still craving their parents' approval? How is it they can't take an appropriate stand or be firm with their parents when they make outrageous demands or behave unacceptably?

In the best scenario, of course, both parent and child are grown up. At this stage in their lives, they enjoy a mature relationship grounded in respect, acceptance, and love. When fear and domination do not exist, their connection can be a genuine friendship without hierarchical boundaries. This is, in essence, the goal of all healthy parent-child relationships.

However, since both parties in intimate long-term relationships are rarely in sync, in all likelihood one party will be grown up, the other not (see Chapter 5). In late-in-life parent-child relationships, specifically, a parent may cling to the role of power while a child is ready to meet that parent as equal; or a child may remain ferociously adolescent, rebelling against everything a parent does, while a parent is willing to yield the high ground. Under these circumstances, the road is strewn with obstacles: a 75-year-old father insists that his son spend Saturday afternoon with him rather than with his girlfriend because he as parent comes first; a 50-year-old daughter still needs to defend to her bigoted father her intermarriage to a Catholic; a 55-year-old son refuses to accept that his 90-year-old mother feels too frail to attend her granddaughter's wedding.

Nevertheless, hope springs eternal as long as one party can behave with wisdom and courage. Whether parent or child, that person has the insight to limit pain and the strength to stand firm. And frequently, his or her maturity and grace will help the other party learn to respect differences and acknowledge that power plays only create emotional distance.

Caregiver, child, and *children*, are words that can be found on just about every page of this book. Although I am satisfied with the term *caregiver* to describe the current helping or supportive role of grown children in regard to their aging parents, I am uncomfortable using the words *child* and *children* to accurately portray the status of caregivers who are well into the fourth, fifth and sixth decades of life. Even prefaced by the words *grown* or *middle-aged*, they are still far from appropriate.

Mid-lifer, middle-ager, parent-carer, and *middle person*, were other terms I experimented with, but they left me dissatisfied. They were awkward, and failed to convey the meaning I was looking for. Even *adult child*, despite its common meaning as adult children of alcoholics, adult children of divorce, and so on, did not fill the bill. If you are a child, how can you be an adult? The term adds confusion rather than clarity to the identity issue.

My problem with finding the right language, however, enabled me to realize two important facts. First, because of the newness of parent care and the corresponding interest in late-life parent-child relationships, the absence of one term to describe these children is understandable. All newly discovered territory requires a name, and someone in the future may just coin a better term. For now, the existing vocabulary will have to do.

Second, the fact is that children in a biological sense remain children as long as they have parents. What happens to children when parents die is somewhat like what happens to a lap when someone stands up—children lose what defines them as children. The difference is that their new status is unchangeable; unlike the lap that reappears upon sitting down, people without parents can never be children again. Since I am writing about people with parents, people who are somebody's children, *child* and *children* will be used throughout this book.

Death does not diminish the mysterious bond between parent and child. We remember what our parents said, the expressions on their faces, the clothes they wore at certain times, the gentle touch of their hands, how they loved their favorite chair, the way they smelled, what they liked to read or see on television, and what made them laugh or cry.

My mother has been dead for seven years, yet, I think of her every day and can still hear her voice in my mind. At times she warns me; other times she may praise, chastise, or shame me. There is no question that her counsel and values still govern much of what I do and say and that her wisdom and stories are part of me. In fact, she is one of the reasons I am writing this book. For had we not made up for the difficult, tumultuous early years of our lives together, my memories of her today would be bitter. During the last 19 years (age 67 to 86) of my mother's life, she and I did the work of making ourselves known to each other. It was then we forged the intimacy that sustains and nourishes me at this very moment. It was then we forgave each other all the unintentional, misguided slights that hurt so much. Of course, I miss her and always will.

My 90-year-old father, in fact, still speaks of *his* mother, dead for well over a half century. He cries because her face has become a blur and because he didn't kiss her good-bye when she asked to be kissed, when at age 20 he left Lithuania for the United States. He still says with deepest sadness, "You see I always thought I would come back, so I didn't kiss her."

And how many times, when I worked as a consultant for a nursing home, did residents sit and talk with me about memories of their parents and what those memories mean. How many times did other residents, bewildered and disoriented from dementia, when the unconscious is fully unveiled, approach me to ask if I could help find their mothers so they could be together again.

We think a lot about our parents—what they did, said, and thought. Indeed, as our current understanding of family dynamics reveals, every intimate relationship we have over the course of our lives reflects in some major way the one we had with our parents. The strength of the bond is so profound that even children who have been abused can care for their elderly parents.

In the same sense, parents who neither like nor love their children still turn to them for help or for some kind of affirmation during the final years of their lives. Parents who swear they would never leave their friends move thousands of miles away from them to live near their children. The push for closeness is relentless, as parents and children try to heal old wounds and understand one another, perhaps for the first and only time. In a cold and impersonal world characterized by increased individual isolation, our connection to our parents is precious.

The fact is, parents and children need one another. By the time parents are in old age and their children in middleage, both parents and their children had better learn to appreciate this need and how to attend to it. Using out-dated rules of how children should behave to determine who is right and what is proper simply doesn't work. Hostility and emotional distance destroy the healthy interdependency of the generations that is important in all stages of life, but crucial during later years.

Each generation makes it hard for the other, failing to learn how to let go and take personal responsibility. Listening to the bitter moans, groans, and criticisms each generation hurls at the other, I shake my head in disbelief at the inability of each to really hear what the other is saying. I want to bang their heads together in hopes of making them realize how much precious time they're wasting.

What can I say to well-intentioned parents and children that will put them on the right road? How can I help them understand that it is never too late to make up for past neglects and misunderstandings? How can I convince children that unless they come to terms with their elderly parents now, their wounds may be recycled into the next generation as they repeat the same patterns with their own children?

Although it may appear that I am suggesting that most parent-child relationships are askew at this crossroads, I am not. Most, in fact, are good. And when they are defined by give and take and respect, they can be infinitely joyous. On the other hand, when they are bad they bring pain and guilt that are hard to wash away.

What I have written consists of a wide range of anecdotal material (based on actual case histories and interviews) on the struggles of parents and children to get it right with each other during the second half of their lives. Wherever appropriate, I have included research on human development that pertains to the aging process, the stages of middle age and old age, and the family in later life. Within all this information there are many guidelines and suggestions for self-help.

What I have learned from counseling and talking to parents and children who have been able to achieve friendship—and from those who have failed—is of great value. Those who have made it despite the poor odds of a troubled history provide both hope and inspiration. Since I selected stories that I felt reflected themes common to most families, I am certain they will ring true for many of my readers. Moreover, I have heard and seen enough fractious elderly parent and middle-aged-child relationships throughout the years to know that even in the closest families certain problems surface. Indeed, everyone of this certain age can benefit from a deeper understanding of the emotional, psychological, and cultural barriers that stand in the way of parents and children loving each other more maturely.

Begining with the first chapter (Why at Fifty-Plus?), I suggest that the potpourri of emotions stirred up by the old age of parents, the middle age of their children, and the spectres of decline, dependence, and death can produce a balm powerful enough to heal generational wounds. I argue that if both parents and children are mature enough (Chapters 2, 3, and 4) to harness the energy of the second half of life—using it to explore new roles and to find healthier ways of relating to one another—they can attain the intimacy that eluded them in earlier stages of their relationship. In fact, this intimacy may be deeper because as adults, both parents and children bring to it the wisdom of experience. Once time is limited, the wisdom of both generations compels them to relate to one another with more compassion and respect.

I also suggest in Chapter 7, where I briefly touch on sociological issues, that if ever there were a time to hammer out new relationship rules it is now. The winds of change are blowing throughout our country. Once untouchable core values and beliefs about family, work, education, and relationships are being questioned. Honesty and openess in all relationships, for example, are considered healthy, leading to more authentic and intimate connections.

Certainly, older parents and their middle-aged children who appreciate these precious years do not want to squander them in fighting ancient battles. They recognize the opportunity afforded by this stage of life to finish old business and resolve lingering conflicts. In whatever time is left to us and no matter how old we are, it is never to late to do the work of becoming wise.

1

Why at Fifty Plus?

Usually there are six of us, including myself. We gather on Tuesday evenings in my dimly lit office to talk about what it's like to be of that certain age when our parents depend on us for care and support. Although I, a clinical social worker, am the professional facilitator of this group, I, too, have an elderly parent to whom I give a certain amount of care. So in a sense, I am part of this group of people. More often than not, our gathering consists of women who are in middle age. Every now and then, a middle-aged man or a younger person may show up, greatly enriching the group. All are welcome. The only criteria for membership is that those who seek out the group for counseling be involved to some extent in caring for an elderly parent or parents. Although I refer to the group and its members throughout this writing, they represent only a small sampling of clients, friends, and others to whom I have spoken and who have sought my help over the last 18 years. With the aged population growing faster than ever, groups similar to this can be found throughout the country. If there is a difference between the focus of my group and others, it lies in the depth in which we explore relationship problems between parent and child. Because of this dimension, the group provides active counseling as well as necessary support.

Over the past 14 years, all kinds of people have taken their place in the group's circle of chairs. We have welcomed nurses, lawyers, computer programmers, professors, salespeople, homemakers, travel agents, teachers, realtors, social workers, and librarians. They have been married, remarried, single, divorced, and widowed and they have represented a wide range of religions. What pulls together these children of a certain age has little to do with their socioeconomic or ethnic background.

They grumble about long waiting lists for nursing homes, the steep cost of home health care, and the chronic loneliness and suffering of their parents, but there are other themes as well. Something is not quite right in their relationship with their elderly parents; pain and animosity exist when the opposite ought to prevail, parent-child relationships are defined by domination and control rather than friendship, and they do not know how to cross the communication barrier to achieve the intimacy and closeness with their parents that they wish.

Children, seemingly grown up, some grandparents and retired, cannot tell their parents what is in their hearts; they are afraid of addressing them as adult to adult. A 59-year-old son, Peter, sums up his confusion and angst this way:

> I feel like a little boy again when my mother starts to give me the business that if I loved her I would see her more than once a week. She always starts every one of our visits with this line. I feel myself shrink into something small and helpless when she starts with this stuff. She also makes me feel that I am a bad and selfish person. I don't know what to say to her. In my head, I know she's wrong and also being abusive in riding me this way. In my heart I think, well, maybe she's right. Maybe I'm not a good son. Although I know I do the best I can, considering how busy I am with my job and my family. It's as if I'm a little boy again, sitting in her kitchen and she's scolding me for not taking out the garbage or throwing my dirty laundry in the hamper. I'm about to be a grandfather in a few weeks, but when she and I are together I'm still a little kid who can't do anything right. Why can't I tell her how I feel; how angry I am at her for treating me like a child. And is this the note on which our relationship will end? It's not what I want. It's not how I want to remember these final years. It's not what I want my grown children to see.

Another grown child whose relationship with her father is hostile and argumentative told the group one evening that after their last telephone conversation, she suddenly realized that, "Suppose my father died right after we said good-bye! We had another one of our colossal battles; we were both angry and upset. And that could have been my final memory of him and our relationship—enough to riddle me with guilt and torment for the rest of my life. How can we get things straight between us once and for all? I really love him but he doesn't know it. And we have so little time to get it right. It's really now or never, and I simply don't know how to talk to him without getting mad."

It is because time is running out that this stage of life is ideal to work on growing up. For elderly parents and their middle-aged children, time is not something to waste. People who are aware of this realize that time exists to heal old wounds, not to open them, to resolve conflicts rather than create new ones, to touch each other with affection and understanding instead of battling over the telephone.

The urgency to resolve unfinished business is a need for both children of that certain age and their parents. Whether at 50, 60, 70, or 80-plus, parents and children want to make it right between them. If not now, when? they ask, knowing that this may be their only opportunity to add to their relationship the love and understanding that has eluded them over the years. Just because reconciliation comes late does not diminish its sweetness. Indeed, the reconciliation is even better when people can appreciate the unique fulfillment of a loving parent-child connection.

Of course, elderly parents are keenly aware that each day may be their last. As life's journey approaches its end, even healthy elderly people take nothing for granted. Most people say what is on their minds at this stage in life, expressing displeasure as easily as affection and gratitude. Said my friend's 82-year-old aunt in horror and dismay to the waiter at a chic restaurant, "*This* is roast chicken! Where are the bones? Don't you know roast chicken *has bones*!" Placing minor indiscretions or worries—like not having the right clothes for a party or agonizing over kitchen walls that need painting—in perspective, they swiftly remind us of the things that really matter—relationships, warmth, the love of family, and friends.

It is now pure delight for me to be with my father, for example. Being free to be open and honest, I always feel that between us there is nothing but truth. A worry over my daughter's life as a single parent is simultaneously affirmed and dismissed with his wise pronouncement that life is hard and things could always be worse. Never minimizing my pain or giving false reassurance, he adds some words about how time changes everything, reminding me of the troubles I gave my mother and him when I was younger. I listen to his wisdom, knowing both that what he says is so and that I will say the same things to my children and grandchildren.

What is often forgotten, however, is that children of elderly parents feel their own stirrings of mortality. As their parents grow old and they watch the physical changes that age carves on their parents' faces and bodies, they also, perhaps for the first time, confront their own death. How strange it is that as long as our parents remain young and healthy, we believe that we will too. When we begin to see their age, we are jarred with an awareness of our own aging. We suddenly take a look at life, realizing that when they die, we move to that indefensible front line where we are completely vulnerable, where our destiny is clearly laid out.

The magic age of 50 produces a state of disquiet on its own. With this half-century birthday something seems to automatically switch on, like a fire alarm when there is intense heat, warning us that the years ahead are fewer than those we already lived. "It seems," said one 60-year-old daughter whose mother has Alzheimer's disease, "that there is this inner voice inside me always saying, 'Pay attention! Take note! Time is at a premium and there's not a minute to waste.' After all, what's to say I won't be like my mother in a few years."

This awareness can give mid-lifers the extraordinary opportunity to feel more alive and to live more fully than at any other time in their lives, and it also prepares them to march into old age without a regretful glance backward. The frequent references to middle-age "crisis" obscures its potential as a time for growth and enriching the mind and spirit.

Mid-life is like a magic box into which we throw many of the old ways, beliefs, and values that have defined our lives. We shake the box around, dump its fragments onto the ground, and, like shamans, scan them for messages and clues about life and the future. What in our lives do we still hold dear? Which relationships do we cherish; which ones seem superficial and not worth maintaining? What values do we find empty and wish to discard? And so the process goes, as we reevaluate and rethink the very meaning of our own lives.

For some people, mid-life reflection can result in changing a job, a spouse, or perhaps both; for others, the end product is a new intimacy with aging parents. Perhaps the main reason for reexamining the parent-child relationship at this time is because it suddenly becomes a large part of the life of the usually middle-aged daughter or son. The health needs of parents now assume great importance in their children's daily lives.

Because middle-aged children are eager to squeeze it all in while their own health and energy are at their peak, they view their parents' need for assistance with ambivalence. Yes, they want to be supportive, but not if it means sacrificing too many of their own plans. With the all-consuming child-rearing years behind them and retirement either in the offing or at hand, they are finally free to live as they please. Taking long vacations, continuing their education, and fulfilling dreams that once were impossible now become tangible realities. Mid-life is a new life. We have enough life experience to sort out the value from the fluff. We know where we want to go; what we want to do.

Yet, we mid-lifers with aging parents all too quickly realize that our long-awaited agendas for fun and personal growth often will not proceed as we envisioned. Our parents' needs for care and assistance intrude.

Fifty-year-old Marie's life was changed by her father's call in the middle of the night to say that her mother'd had a stroke. Traveling to Florida from New Jersey every other month to check on support services, Marie now has little time for her grandchildren and those pleasurable activities she once enjoyed.

When her chronically ill father moved in with Pearl, 60, and her newly retired husband, it marked the end of their dreams of vacations in their camper and frequent visits with their children and grandchildren on the West Coast. Pearl and her husband joined an ever-growing group. Nearly one-third of people in the United States who are approaching retirement age have responsibility for an aging parent or parent-in-law.[1]

Lilly, 52, a professor of English Literature at a large university, represents the effects of caregiving on the life of a single woman without children. She is the eldest daughter in a family of five, the rest of whom are married. Lilly's 80-year-old mother opted to move near her as she became disabled and frail because she believed that Lilly's life was less complicated than her brothers' and sisters', and the family thought the move made sense. In the three years that Lilly's mother has lived near her, however, her caregiving responsibilities have forced Lilly to turn down a deanship and a summer fellowship to study abroad, and now she wonders if she will have to sacrifice her sabbatical. Single grown children also have lives to live. The era of the maiden aunt who cared for aging parents is gone forever. Currently, most children of a certain age work, and many have numerous responsibilities and live frantically full lives.

Of course, we all knew that our parents would grow old, but we expected it to occur with more favorable timing and greater consideration for our own needs. How dare our parents get old so suddenly, without advance warning, without giving us time to reach our mid-life goals! How dare Mom have a stroke! Why couldn't Dad live on his own for just a few more years? Why does Mom need me to take care of her instead of my brothers and sisters? With what seems like the speed of lightning, our parents need us much more than we need them. Suddenly, grown children become caregivers, turning their lives upside down for years to come.

For many children, the death of one parent causes the transformation from passively concerned middle-aged son or daughter to actively concerned, if not outright worried, caregiver. A daughter may be shocked at how the death of her father disrupts her life. Never suspecting that her mother was dependent and attention-seeking because her father acted as a buffer, she probably was unaware of her mother's emotional needs. Helpless to fend off her mother's relentless bids for attention and without a father to shield her, she feels like she is suddenly on the front line. On one hand, she feels sorry for Mother because she is now alone; on the other, she is furious because her mother depends on her for everything rather than making the effort to cultivate new friends and interests. What was previously a peaceful coexistence deteriorates within a year into one defined by tension and bitterness. Beth, 52, comments on what is an all-too-typical problem: "When my mother became a widow, I expected her to carve out a life for herself with her friends. She was a healthy 73-year-old at the time, bright and sociable. What I found out, though, was that my father was the lifeline to her world. Without him, she was paralyzed. So now, she wants my husband and me to be her entertainment. Why she even tried to wriggle her way into our last vacation."

However grown children become caregivers, they usually find themselves on a collision course with their parents. The needs of one generation conflict with the needs of the other, and unless both parties are grown up, the process of trying to negotiate a solution often leads to turmoil. Even in the most warm, communicative, and loving families, there is an uneasiness at this critical point.

Increased longevity is a modern phenomenon that has not been around long enough for the formulation of rules and norms to guide us. As a result, even well-intentioned parents and children experience confusion and conflict that may result in anger. Something as minor as a weekly aerobics class prompted a heated argument between Angela, an only child, and her 75-year-old mother, Kaye, when her mother's doctor's appointment fell on the same morning as the class. Her mother fully expected Angela to take her to the doctor because until she became wise, Angela was her mother's faithful servant. She became furious when Angela told her she had to take care of herself that day. Her mother, incredulous over Angela's frivolous reason, clearly believed it meant her daughter did not love her and was not devoted to her. They were able to patch up their differences without lasting damage, however, because of their warm underlying relationship and because Kaye appreciated Angela's help in finding her a new home near Angela and moving her in after her husband died. In fact, the aerobics conflict enabled them to reach a clearer, more realistic understanding of what each expected from the other.

There is enough sustained emotional interaction between parent and child in caregiving to help them understand the ties that bind them together, and sometimes unravel. It makes sense to look at caregiving as a context in which to explore what happens when parents age and need their middle-aged children for support. Not only do the old, dysfunctional ways of their relationship resurface, they are also more powerful. They are like tire tracks that have been driven on over and over again, with deeply rutted patterns and details of every tread etched in sharp relief.

Children who have spent their lives fearfully reacting to their parents' intimidation become more fearful and intimidated at this stage. Children who sought but never gained approval seek it more tenaciously. Children who were dutiful become more solicitous. Children who never liked their parents like them even less. It's old history playing itself out again. But now skirmishes are battles where lives, or at least what remains of them, are at stake. And the time to smooth and soothe is running out.

Because the fragility of parents in old age is a powerful tool for manipulation, children often become more timid about speaking up for their own needs. What I often hear is, How can I tell my mom, who is old and not well, something that will hurt her feelings? After all, how long can she live? So it's okay if she has her way and I hold my tongue. And because parents who related to their younger children through domination become even more autocratic with age, they only make their children's childish fears worse. They know no other way. Forcing their children to become compliant, leaving no room for the authentic expression of emotions or spontaneity, they foster an oppressive relationship where no one is free to be his or her real self. Although the cast of characters is the same in this rerun of family history, the weaknesses and strengths of both parties seem to have grown disproportionately big.

Grown children talk about the pain they experience while trying to do right by their parents and still live their own lives. They tell me how much they want friendship and understanding. Yet their best intentions and all they do are never quite enough, with parents demanding more than they can realistically give. Their parents don't seem to believe that they care, nor do they understand how complex their children's lives are. When they hark back to when their own parents were old and use this as a standard for the present, parents not only make their children feel guilty, they increase emotional estrangement. Most of all, children worry that the good memories they have of their parents will be tarnished in these later years.

Ironically, elderly parents feel the same pain and sadness. More poignantly aware of the shortness of time, they are often eager to heal old wounds and resolve long-standing conflicts. The problem is they simply don't know how to go about doing it. The terrain is confusing because the old signposts directing parent-child relationships are no longer relevant. "Parents are always parents and children always children," they steadfastly intone; yet, something is not quite right. Yes, their children are still their children, but they have changed over time. Not only are they "big" and becoming gray and wrinkled, but they have become smarter and more savvy about life. Their wisdom comes as a surprise to parents who forget that their children are also rapidly becoming elders.

How do parents correlate this growth and sophistication with the old rules about relationships passed down to them by their parents? What does "honor thy father and mother" mean when children are too busy to visit every week or call every day? Or when some live so far away that months go by without seeing them face to face? What does "honor thy father and mother" mean when a child tells a parent she does not want her advice on how to raise her children? And what does "honor thy father and mother" mean when children say they cannot invite an elderly parent to move in with them?

Elderly parents still have a lot to figure out. They feel like parents and they *are* parents, but something has changed. What they may find so impossible to understand is that modern times are dramatically different from the days when their own parents were old. For one thing, people died at an earlier age back then. For another, daughters—the traditional caregivers of our society—usually remained home without the many responsibilities they face today. I did it for my parents without fuss, so why can't my children do the same for me, seems to be the lingering cry. Or as a 70-year-old friend has repeatedly asked me, "How come I worry about my children and they don't seem to worry about me?" They are expressing their doubts and anxieties over whether their children really care.

It's true that parents never stop being parents. They worry and question their children's decisions until the day they die. A child's divorce is their pain too; a child's failure to succeed in school or at work is also their heartache. This, however, does not give parents the right to intrude into their children's lives without permission or to assume they always know what is best.

The authoritarian tone some parents use to express what they consider to be their prerogatives doesn't sit well. The fact is, their children are now *adults*. Living their own lives, fighting their own battles, and raising their own children, grown children wish to be accepted and respected as their parents' equals in worth and status. The old rules on how sons and daughters should behave no longer apply. Parents are left wondering what they can do to bridge a generation gap that is widening at a time when there *is* no time.

"What can I do to make things better between my mother and me? How do I even begin to talk to her?" asked an intelligent and sensitive 49-year-old woman who attended a class I presented entitled, "Parents, Children, and Aging." A nurse, obviously warm and compassionate, she told the class she and her 71-year-old mother relate like polite strangers. Every time she asks her mother what it's like to be in pain from arthritis and to be alone most of the day, her mother responds with, "I'm doing just fine, dear." She felt that perhaps her mother was trying to protect her, but realized that in doing so she was depriving her of the opportunity to really get to know her mother as a person and to help her. After all, she was a trained nurse. Before I could open my mouth to respond, the vibrant 70-year-old in the next chair, looking her squarely in the eyes, said, "Better talk to your mother—and *now*—because you don't know how much time is left. Just tell her that you feel strange with her; that you know she's trying to protect you, but that's not what you want. Tell it how you feel it—straight from the heart, that's all! Your mother sounds as if she's afraid of something, probably of getting close. Maybe she was hurt by her parents when she was little, I don't know. But don't you be scared. She'll thank you for opening the floodgates."

Janice, a 44-year-old daughter whose 80-year-old mother had been living with her for two years, poignantly illustrates the critical role of time in forging closeness between elderly parents and their grown children. A successful physician and mother of two toddler daughters, she related the following story:

> I asked my mother to move in with my family, as I felt this would be our last chance to work out some unfinished business between us. I am an only child. My father died when I was 16 and I was truly my father's daughter. He and I had a close relationship. While he was alive, whatever problems my mother and I had receded into the background because of his warm and giving presence. After he died, everything changed. My mother was angry; she took her anger out on me; every day in that house was torment. I did not want to be

around her because she was so verbally abusive and very strict as far as my social life was concerned. Finally, I went away to college and after that I rarely came home except for holidays. When I was in medical school and later during my residency, I was busy enough to have an excuse to be home even less.

Three years ago she had a stroke, and her vision, due to macular degeneration, rendered her unable to live on her own. Believing that I now had a chance to make up for all those years of hostility and emotional distance, I asked her to move in with us. Well, she's still critical and nasty and every time I reach out to her, she slaps me right down. So, I've stopped trying to be nice. I don't need her rejection and what surprises me is that I am still terrified of her. She still has the power to make me feel like an inadequate and helpless child.

Oddly enough, though, I still keep thinking there's hope for us, if only I knew how to go about getting her to talk to me. Her sister, my aunt, who came to spend a long weekend with us, told me my mother would like to do something to lessen the tension between us. Besides what my aunt says, my mother really worships her two granddaughters. And I feel they may be the conduit to reconciliation.

With all my heart, I don't want our relationship to end with all these bad feelings between us. And my mother is frail with some serious medical problems. How long can she last? I am literally in torment over the state of our relationship. I keep thinking about how guilty I will feel after she dies.

Here they are, mother and daughter, two adults, both wanting closeness and meaningful connection, with neither knowing how to obtain it. Janice, successful in her profession, resourceful and emotionally giving as a mother, and comfortable in other significant relationships, remains stymied by her mother's intimidation and control. Fearing rejection but wanting desperately to finally make it right, she resigns herself to avoiding any heart-to-heart talk. She feels that the situation holds hope because of her mother's love for her granddaughters and from the information her aunt has given her about her mother's thoughts on their relationship.

Grandchildren are, indeed, one of the major reasons why elderly parents push for cordial relationships with their grown children. Janice was afraid it was too late to make peace with her mother, and it was, because her mother died six months after our conversation. Janice's children, however, did make a slight difference during the last months of Janice's mother's life. Using the granddaughters as a springboard to conversations about immortality, Janice was able to get her mother to open up. Asking her questions about how she wanted to be remembered after her death, Janice and her mother at least touched upon the meaning of their own troubled relationship. Although each was able to say some forgiving words to the other, not enough was said to bridge their differences and create understanding. Today, Janice remains haunted by bitter memories of her mother, wishing she had acted sooner to break the communication barrier that separated them. As she wondered aloud to me if she would ever be able to lessen the guilt that tore at her or be able to come to terms with her mother, I remembered the all-too-true words of the protagonist in Robert Anderson's drama, *I Never Sang for My Father*: "Death ends a life but it doesn't end a relationship."[2]

Grandchildren can be an important reason why grandparents try to reach an accord with their children, but the central force in most grown-child and elder-parent relationships is power. This element is directly confronted within the framework of caregiving.

There is a reversal of power as parents age. The fact is that older children do not need their parents as they did when they were young, but their parents need them more. (The exception is disabled children, addressed in Chapter 6, for whom dependence on parents may always be necessary.) As family therapist Lee Headley points out, however, this shift does not mean that a child's newly acquired power is to be spent in exploiting a parent's vulnerabilities.[3] Just as a healthy parent never abuses a child's trust, neither do healthy caregiving children. Unfortunately, elder abuse has become a horrible reality in our country. In this, children try to avenge past hurts and grievances by behaving cruelly and sometimes violently toward their parents. It does not pertain to the parents and children I write about in this book.

Unlike children who abuse their power, the children we classify as grown up can understand and accept a parent's aging and are there for emotional and physical support as much as they can be. Indeed, to be a mature son or daughter, the grown child ought to wield power compassionately, with care and empathy for a parent's needs and feelings.[4]

Parents, too, have a tough row to hoe. They must realize that parental domination has a statute of limitations. Specifically, does the 78-year-old mother have the right to tell her daughter that if she truly cared about her she would have her over to dinner more than once a week? Does she have right to tell her she owes her this because of her unending sacrifices to raise her? Pushing sensitive guilt buttons is risky. This just causes pain and resentment. Parents must recognize that their children can never pay them back for all they did; that the concept of owing (See Chapter 6) is not a part of parenting. Is this the reason we raise children? For reward? There are deeper satisfactions for parents who have the good sense to toss out guilt from their relations with their grown children. They rely instead upon healthier ways to foster closeness and understanding.

During a question-and-answer period following one of my talks to people involved with the care of an elderly parent, a 62-year-old woman stood up to comment about what it was like for her and her husband to live with her 80-year-old mother. Sounding more like a helpless child than a grown woman, but with a poignant despair that commanded immediate attention, she told the audience in graphic detail what parental power is all about at this turning point in the life of the family:

> My mother has been living with us for almost four years. She is healthy in mind and body and will probably outlive both my husband and me, because she is not bashful about making demands for her own health and well-being.
>
> She refuses to let us go out alone, insisting she has a right to be with us at all times. We cannot go out to dinner, to visit friends, or to see a movie. Sunday we all went to Atlantic City together. After lunch, my husband and I wanted to walk along the boardwalk to one of our favorite ice cream places. She did not want to join us, preferring instead to play the slot machines at one of the casinos, and we thought we were finally off the hook. But . . . when we told her we would probably be gone for at least two hours and would pick her up around 3:30, she told us that wouldn't do. That *she* wasn't going to wait for *us*; we could wait for her but not the other way around. And besides if she had come on the bus with her senior group, the bus would be there at least a half hour earlier. Well, we went for our walk, always looking at our watches, always rushing. We got back there at exactly 3 o'clock, you can be sure!

By this time, the woman was in tears, and the audience was trans-
fixed by her words. I asked her husband, who was sitting next to
her, what would happen if the next time they straightforwardly told
Mother they were going off to Atlantic City without her because
they wanted time alone. The husband instantly replied, "We could
never do that. She wouldn't like that at all. She'd pout and be angry
with us for days and weeks to come. We couldn't live with her that
way." His final remarks were, "It's really sad not to be free. We're
getting on too, you know. If we don't live now, then when?" These
valedictory words go right to the heart of the matter.

The fact that people, like the previous couple, are living longer
and in most cases healthier lives also forces parents and children to
learn to relate to each other maturely. Nowadays, parents 80 and
90 years of age have children in their 60s and 70s. In fact, 3 percent of children over 70 have a surviving parent.[5] It is common
today to see a 72-year-old daughter visiting her 90-year-old mother
in the nursing home. Even more appropriate to what we are saying
is to see them dining out or shopping together.

Although time is running out for each generation, the amount of
time parents and children spend together as adults has actually
increased. At this juncture, too, chronological age blurs as a differ-
entiating factor. Both parent and child are now adults who "share
many of the same ego, social, sexual, and power needs common to
the adult years of life."[6] For example, both generations may well
have experienced divorce, widowhood, remarriage, the death of a
child, and financial reversal. By now, both recognize the importance
of loving relationships in their daily lives. At this stage of the game,
with both generations having tasted life's disappointments and joys,
they possess all the ingredients necessary for a rich friendship.

Furthermore, 10 to 15 years spent squabbling over love and
devotion based on outdated hierarchic parent-child roles can seem
like an eternity of self-induced hell. Norman Mailer had it right
when he said in an interview in the *New York Times*, "The kids are
grown up, so a good deal of my social life is with the kids. I have
nine kids, and it's amazing how much social life that gives you."[7]

Besides the obvious constraints of time, another reason for these
changes at this time of life lies in the nature of our complex, fre-
netic world, where middle-aged women make up a large part of
the work force. *Sandwich generation*, the popular term for grown

children caught between the needs of their parents and the needs of their spouses and children, hardly seems adequate. With the addition of the third layer, work, *club sandwich* is more apt.

Pulled in all directions, caregivers hardly know where to run first or who comes first. They ask themselves, Is it okay to have lunch with my best friend when my father would like to be with me? Am I selfish in wanting to visit my grandchildren when my mother would like me to take her grocery shopping? How can I possibly make my mother understand that I would just like to have a weekend to myself instead of bringing her to my house yet another time? These questions did not pop into the heads of Moses' followers when he read the Fifth Commandment, ordering them to honor their mothers and fathers. Nor were they pertinent at the turn of the twentieth century. Back then, women were not burdened with multiple responsibilities, including jobs, nor did significant numbers of their parents live long enough to require the prolonged care that chronic illness demands.

If ever there was a time for new rules and clear communication between elderly parents and their children, it is now. Today's rapidly changing world demands that we take a new look at beliefs and traditions that once were considered sacred.

Changes in the structure of the family also affect what happens between parents and their grown-up children. With step- and single-parent families outnumbering traditional ones, many grown children are faced with additional responsibilities that often conflict with their parents' needs. A 43-year-old caregiver working part-time as a graphics designer describes how her life as a remarried woman meshes with her 78-year-old father's needs for emotional support.

> Though I love and care about my Dad, I cannot see him as much as I would like. I remarried a man with two children a little over a year ago and I have two kids myself. You can just imagine how pressured I am. My first priority is to try to forge us into one family. He does not understand this, and it seems I cannot make him see what my life now is about. I've told him how sorry I am, that I care for him and know he's lonely, but that I can only spend just so much time with him now. He's really disappointed in me as a daughter, telling me he expected more. It's sad beyond words to think that at this time of our lives we are experiencing conflict. And that we might not be able to work things out.

Because we're all shouldering more responsibilities than we can manage and because the family structure is so different today, the issue of how sons and daughters behave is forced to its limit. Rabbi Cary Kozberg, director of rabbincal and patoral services at Wexner Heritage Village in Columbus, Ohio, eloquently coveys the heart of the predicament in the following statement: "As moderns, we live lifestyles which are much more complicated and demanding than those of our ancestors—lifestyles which often confuse rather than clarify just what our obligations to elderly parents really are, lifestyles which may hinder rather than help us determine just how we may appropriately fulfill them."[8]

Janice's story not only illustrates the painful consequences of unresolved issues, but also how critical time is at this juncture in family life. An individual can surely come to terms with a parent's psychological abuse or achieve inner peace after a parent has died. Perhaps Janice will be lucky enough to be such a person. There are, however, unique benefits to negotiating these tasks while parents remain active in their children's lives.

When a parent and child are both living, they can confront each other face to face, and see the truth in what they believe or dismiss old ideas. Either way, the result is clarity and the possibility of forgiveness.

An adult son and only child, Jerry felt worthless in the eyes of his perfectionist and driven physician-father. The pressure on Jerry to please his father was always intense. Because he was interested in a career in journalism rather than medicine, however, he deeply disappointed his father. After finishing college and marrying, Jerry returned home only every other Christmas. His father was still smarting from his son's career choice and let Jerry know how hurt and angry he was whenever he visited, so Jerry and his wife decided the less Jerry saw of his father the better. The pattern continued despite the efforts of Jerry's mother to heal the relationship, until Jerry's father was in his 70s and dying of cancer. Two weeks before his death, his father told Jerry how sorry he was for his abusive and demeaning behavior. He said he wished he had come to his senses earlier and that he respected Jerry for who and what he is. He said he hoped Jerry would forgive "a very foolish and unwise old man."

Take the case of a 69-year-old mother who said the following to her 45-year-old daughter after she finally summoned up the courage to say she felt unloved and not as favored as her younger sister: "No, I never favored her over you and I am truly sorry you felt this way all these years. I can certainly understand why you thought that, but I always loved you and thought you a remarkable and giving child. But you see, you were always more capable than your sister was; you seemed so independent and not to need as much as she. So I gave her more love and attention than you, because I felt you were the stronger."

If a relationship can't be healed because one person is too stubborn to forgive, then the other will at least have tried. He or she will have done as much as humanly possible and must accept the result, partial though it is. The key is to realize the rejection is not personal but that the other party's injuries are at the core. A child, for example, can accept a parent as he or she is, grieve for a relationship that was never meant to be as he or she wished, and go on with life.

Relations between elderly parents and their children are stressed today. The proliferation of literature and the growth of support groups such as CAPS (Children of Aging Parents) throughout the country indicate that this is a problem that is becoming even more widespread.[9] These developments also clearly show that children and parents want to enhance and enrich their bond; to build their relationship on understanding, not anger and guilt.

The goal, when possible, is to make the "bad" less bad and perhaps even "good," and to make the "good" better. The urgency of time affects the ties that bind, giving both generations the courage they need to confront and finally acknowledge each other as adults who care and want to be close. Because there is not a minute to waste and so many deeply gratifying rewards may result, this stage of life becomes both a challenge and an opportunity.

The answer to the question, Why at fifty plus? is no puzzle. It is the last chance elderly parents and their children have to finish their business with love, respect, and empathy. Holding, touching, talking, as adults bound by ties both mysterious and real, they can get it straight between them once and for all.

2

What's Growing Up All About, Anyway?

What does it mean to be grown up? Does it mean the capacity to stand alone in the face of life's inevitable disappointments and tragedies? To be a sort of superbeing akin to Ayn Rand's fictional hero, Howard Roark, who confronts the lonely world without help from a single soul?[1] Does it mean complete separation from family? When adults need their parents for love, affirmation, and support, are they less than adult?

If we can say "yes" to all or some of these questions, then we are still lost in the wilds of adolescence, where rebellion against parents and what they represent is an indication of adulthood. To grow up, we do psychologically move away from parents, but this kind of distancing is not the same as deliberate rebellion.

Separation-individuation is a term for the process which we achieve identity.[2] This theory suggests that we move through several stages of separation until we reach the final stage, separation-individuation, at which point we become autonomous individuals. While this theory went unchallenged for quite some time, it is currently in question because it emphasizes separation and ignores connection. Although we must separate and become individuals to develop our own unique personalities, our drive for attachment is part of the essential nature of humaness.

By underplaying the importance of connection while promoting the notion of gradual separation from parents, the theory neglects the natural interdependence of parents and children. While it touches on the need small children have to keep returning to their parents for security (*rapprochement*), it does not consider this a mutual process that unfolds throughout the time children and parents spend together. For as long as both generations are alive they return to each other or come into each others' lives. The parent-child bond is the strongest there is. As family therapist James Framo pointedly reminds us, " . . . no one ever really gives up the yearning for the love and acceptance of parents. . . . to be alone or pushed out of the family either physically or psychologically is too unthinkable. . . . Adults, too, require specific reciprocal identities in their intimate others in order to maintain their own identities."[3]

Children and parents remain connected to each other throughout their lives. And as I noted in the previous chapter in the story of Janice and her mother, the attachment does not end with death.

For many reasons, parents and children need each other at all stages of their lives. The nature of this interdependence changes with time, with the once-necessary protective parent up there and dependent child below evolving into more appropriate relationships. The end product of growing up is not nor should it be total independence from parents and what they symbolize. To be more concise, the interdependence of parents and children in one form or another is a fact of life. The goal is to base that interdependence on reciprocity and respect rather than intimidation and control.

Not long ago, Michael, a bright, well-spoken 51-year-old sales executive told me how he successfully cut his mother out of his life. With considerable smugness over his achievement that could not for an instant conceal his underlying anger, he related the following:

> I can never remember liking my mother. She was basically not a nice person. I used to feel disloyal saying this, but I do not anymore. I never felt loved by her, and whatever she did for me was always on her terms. She was never there for me when I needed her. She was verbally abusive, ice cold, and a rotten parent. Although she practically ruined my older sister's life, I made up my mind not to allow her to destroy mine. My sister was and still is frightened to death of her, and so is her husband. They live near her and since my father died, my mother has become even more demanding and selfish. I was determined, as soon as I was able, to get as far away from her as possible. I moved to the East Coast, 3,000 miles from her,

and speak and write to her only on birthdays, holidays, or when someone has died. I consider myself totally emancipated from her and her influence and can honestly say I experience no guilt whatsoever over our divorce.

Believe, if you will, that Michael dislikes and even hates his mother. Believe that what he tells you about her character and personality are true. Believe, too, that physically, 3,000 miles worth, anyway, he has detached from her. But that he is "totally emancipated" from her, *never*! She will enter his thoughts when he least expects it. She will become a yardstick against which he can measure how different he is from her. He will, in fact, in one way or another always be comparing: I am more giving than she is, I am warmer and more loving than she is, I am fairer than she is, I am more thoughtful of others than she is.

Above all, Michael will celebrate these differences. He will need to tell others so they can give credit to his glorious adulthood. Indeed, the more he shouts, "I am free of her" and the more he fights to be unlike her, the more she becomes a framework for his adult development; the more she becomes a powerful force in his life.

And with all Michael's protests that he is fully emancipated, free of his mother, and his own person at last, his anger remains. No matter how blase he tries to be when he talks about her, it comes through. Seething below his cool surface, its energy tells us more than anything else can how powerfully he is still tied to his mother. Make no mistake, there are many ways to remain attached to parents and anger is as mighty a form as any. Although unwholesome, destructive, and adolescent, it nevertheless inexorably links children and parents.

And what of elderly parents? What of those mothers and fathers who believe that to be grown up is to stand alone without their children's support or friendship? What of those mothers and fathers who keep their children at bay by dangling parental authority over their heads? Aren't they also lost in the wilderness of adolescence? Aren't they also missing out on wholesome interdependence?

They are, indeed, as lost and rebellious as their offspring. Just because they are old does not mean they are wise. Literature and real life are filled with plenty of old fools, whose foolishness takes on an extra layer of tragedy in the wake of their advanced years. Maturity has more to do with how elderly parents adapt to and integrate the inevitable losses of old age than the advent of old age itself.

Parents who are mature acknowledge their need for connection and reciprocity. Wise enough to relinquish the parental scepter and welcome their children as equals into their kingdom, they bring about the friendship they desire. Wise enough as well to know that unless they encourage connection now, it may be too late, they do not waste a minute in getting the process of reconciliation started.

Sarah, a 75-year-old widow, was a client of mine for almost three years—one of the increasing number of elderly seeking psychotherapy. Like Michael, she thought she did not need connection with her children. Beginning each session with the same diatribes against her son and daughter, Sarah would have me believe that she really ousted them from her life. Her litany of their misdeeds and misdemeanors, sounding like an official proclamation of grievances, grew in force as time passed. Her daughter never calls; her son, who's rich, sends flowers but never money; they don't invite her to their homes; her daughter is ungrateful for all she did for her over the years; her daughter is selfish; her son is a snob. After venting her wrath, her final words were usually in this vein: "I really don't need them anyway, so why should I be the one to call them. It's their place to call me, anyway. And besides, whenever we do get together we have a terrible time, especially my daughter and me. Thank God, I can manage without them. It's not easy, but I have enough to make it and that's what counts. I really don't have to depend on them for anything."

Does Sarah really not need her children? No. Although she would be hard put to admit it, she knows deep down that her life would be richer and a lot less lonely if they were emotionally connected. What Sarah wants from her children—more than financial or some other form of concrete assistance—is the assurance that she still matters to them and that they want her company. What Sarah wants are the love, affection, and strokes that are so special because they are given by her children. She hungers for this precious involvement with them and their families. Aware that time is short, she would, if only she knew how, do anything to reconnect with them. With a little guidance, Sarah realized that she couldn't afford to wait for her daughter to make the first move. Finally growing up at 75, she picked up the telephone to call her. The details of Sarah's big leap will be described in detail in Chapter 4.

What must be remembered for now is that the "Michaels" are never really independent of their parents and the "Sarahs" never independent of their children. They are always a part of each other's lives in one form or another, and the idea of cut-off is merely an illusion.

For Michael, growing up means recognizing his mother as an integral part of his life. She provides him with connection to the past, with its roots and beginnings and with large chunks of his identity. No matter how geographically distant he is from his mother, they are part of each other. He cannot escape this powerful emotional linkage. After some painful introspection he and his mother would see that, like all human beings, they are neither all bad or all good. To remain angry at her for being human is the same as being angry at himself for being human. That may be what his rumblings are about, anyway.

In Michael's case, I received a call from him a year after we spoke, telling me that his sister was critically ill and he was flying to the West Coast to plan for his mother's long-term care. Though the bond with his mother was non-existent from his perspective, it was strong enough to draw him home to her in her hour of need. When I asked him later how he would have felt if he not gone to his mother's assistance, he replied without a second's hesitation, "Guilty as hell!"

Was the incentive for Michael's action pure moral obligation? I don't think so. To dismiss it as such not only dilutes the parent-child bond but makes it purely mechanical. Of course, some facets of our connection to our parents are rooted in moral imperative. The core of this connection, however, is deeper and much more complex. Composed of thousands of shared experiences, interactions, impressions, memories, thoughts, and feelings, this bond radiates a power that is felt our whole lives long. Despite their long, rancorous relationship, Michael is almost compelled to be with his mother. Even if she cannot give him the affirmation that he is a "good" son, by being with her during her time of crisis he is able to give it to himself.

"I *need* to be with my mother!" said Sheila of her several yearly visits to her 83-year-old mother, who has Alzheimer's and lives in a nursing home 1,000 miles from her home. "Friends ask me why I go at all," she continues, "since my mother hasn't recognized me in two years. They think I'm crazy. How can I not, I answer them. She's my mother. Even if someone told me I didn't have to go, I'd still go. She brought me into this world. I can't just wash my hands of her! I still send her Mother's Day cards, even though she hasn't been able to make sense of them in three years." Moral imperative?

In Sarah's case, she needs her children not only for the emotional goodies but for that sense of belonging to her children's family. Her life, disconnected from them, has become sterile over the years. Bereft of family celebrations, news, and gossip, Sarah feels isolated and abandoned. She is frequently depressed or suffers from some undiagnosed lower back problem. Although she is sociable, with friends and many acquaintances, she is deprived of interaction with her kinfolk and feels her life has lost meaning.

Though in her 70s, Sarah has not grown up. Before she can be considered one of the wise, she must recognize and accept her dependence upon her children. She must acknowledge her need for them to sweeten her days, to warm her heart, and to give her the gift of ongoing life through connection with her grandchildren.

What interdependence of the generations means, essentially, is that parents and children are always as one. When old age arrives, Sarah and other parents will turn to their children for what they can give and do, whether they like their children or not. Likewise, Michael, whether he likes his mother or not, is compelled to complete his task if not with love, then with maturity. It is the nature of this psychological interdependence that parents and children must acknowledge in order to call themselves grown up.

Even in the face of distance, hostility, and abuse, the bond remains tight when tested. The hero of Pat Conroy's novel, *The Prince of Tides*, describes the bond's tensility in these pointed words: "In families there are no crimes beyond forgiveness."[4] Perhaps Robert Frost said it best in his poem, "Death of the Hired Man." In writing about the meaning of home, he described it as "the place where, when you have to go there, they have to take you in."[5] Home and family, then, are one. It is that place, that group, those people that provide unconditional love, support, and frienship.

To be grown up, then, is for parents and children to affirm their connection to each other. It is not to say, I don't need them—I can stand on my own two feet. It is rather to proclaim, of course, I can stand on my own! But this is not the point. I do need them because they are part of my life; they provide me with a connection no one else can; they give me the pieces that make my life whole; their warmth and love enrich my existence.

The expressions, "Grow up, will you" or "he's really so grown up," are used frequently enough in our culture to merit examination. In the first instance, "grow up" is used almost like a command, telling someone to act his or her age and to quit behaving like a child. In the second, "grown up" is used as praise, commending a child for maturity. Although the tone of each context is different, the essence of growing up remains the same.

Accepting responsibility for one's actions, displaying appropriate behavior, demonstrating respect for another's sensibilities, and having a healthy portion of self-esteem are the hallmarks of someone truly grown up. The person who usually finds someone or some circumstance to blame for his or her lot in life cannot be considered adult. The individual who whines or rants rather than articulating his or her feelings has not left the world of nursery school. People who hurt or use others without a flicker of conscience or who allow others to hurt or demean them also have a long way to go to be considered mature.

Within the context of this chapter and this book, all these descriptions are relevant and will be referred to frequently. Among all these issues, self-esteem is primary.

To be grown up means being able to like yourself; to accept yourself completely, including what makes you cringe in shame and what makes you glow with pride. I like to envision self-esteem as something that sends out rays of sunshine telling us that come what may, we are okay; we are "good eggs." In her book, *Revolution from Within*, Gloria Steinem refers to self-esteem as "the one true inner voice."[6]

The late Virginia Satir, however, says it best in her book, *The New Peoplemaking*. The gist of her message lies in these sentences:

> . . . . persons who love and value themselves are able to value others. When one cares for oneself, one will not do anything to injure, degrade, humiliate, or otherwise destroy oneself or another, and

will not hold others responsible for one's actions. The more one values oneself, the less one demands from others. The less one demands from others, the more one can feel trust. The more one trusts oneself and others, the more one can feel trust. The more one trusts oneself and others, the more one can love. The more one knows another, the greater is one's bond and bridge with them."[7]

Without a sense of self-worth, which enables us to feel that we deserve to take care of our whole selves and to stand up for what we feel when we believe we are right, we are always at the mercy of others. Consequently, not only do we feel others are better, smarter, or more lovable, but we believe that our thoughts, feelings, values, beliefs, fantasies, and needs, simply do not matter. Submerging our identity just to please someone means we are not being true to ourselves. Although achieving complete self awareness takes a lifetime, to live with wisdom requires enough self-esteem, enough inner-strength to meet life's setbacks.

Among the hundreds of caregiving children I have counseled, many struggle with issues of self-esteem. Outwardly they appear successful and "together," taught as they were at an early age to believe that style is more important than substance. In their relationships with their parents, however, they remain mired somewhere in childhood. Feeling they have no right to confront their parents as adults, they know in their hearts that they have little self-worth. Despite other noteworthy achievements, they are still compelled to play the role of the ideal, eager-to-please person their parents raised them to be.

Now, ostensibly grown up but still unable to negotiate with their parents on the basis of their current responsibilities and needs, they cannot assert themselves or say "no" when necessary to an outrageously unrealistic demand.

Exclaimed Ellen, 48, a successful sales representative for a large clothing firm: "I can't tell my mother that because I have a fever, I will not take her shopping. I'm never supposed to get sick; I'm simply not allowed. My mother trained me to be invincible. Why, I hardly ever missed a day of school. With this as my background, do you really believe my mother would accept such a lame excuse? She'd be absolutely furious with me. Who needs it? Forget it, I'll take her shopping."

So, rather than heed her body's clear need for rest, and on the basis of an irrelevant, archaic script, Ellen plays out the "good-child-daughter" role her mother expects. She winds up taking her shopping in addition to going to work and caring for her own family. What ultimately happens is that Ellen comes down with a serious case of bronchitis, is bedridden for days, and blames her mother instead of herself for her stress and poor health.

Ellen, like many grown children who lack self-esteem, is fearful that an honest statement of her needs would create an emotional flare-up she could not handle. In her job as well as within her marriage, her inability to stand up for what she feels is right for herself has been a continual concern. Ellen was at last forced to confront her poor sense of self—always brushed aside or lightly acknowledged—within the most fitting place of all: the confines of her relationship to her mother.

Rather than risk an adult interaction with her mother where she just might be heard and have her health needs met, Ellen opts to do it all. The hitch, of course, is that Ellen's compliant response does not solve what has been and will continue to be an ongoing problem. Mother will make additional requests to which Ellen will give in. Ellen will become angry and stressed again, and in all likelihood she will again become ill. Behaving like a powerless little girl, she feels she has lost control of her adult life. And, indeed, without the self-esteem necessary to validate her right to take care of herself, she has. Mired in a dysfunctional morass that only grows stickier, she realizes she must assume the personal responsibility necessary to make her free. (See Chapter 5.)

Children without self-esteem usually have parents without self-esteem. Parents without self-esteem usually were children without self-esteem. Without sufficient love or affection from *their* parents, they reach adulthood wounded and emotionally empty. Fearful of being abandoned and unable to trust their children's commitment to their welfare, the only way they know of having their needs met is through intimidation and control. Their requests and comments become demands and innuendos couched in the language of emotional blackmail: If you really loved me, you wouldn't leave me alone so much; you always think of your wife and yourself but never of me; you go out and have a good time, I never do; after all I did for you, the least you could do is invite me to your beach house for the entire summer; or I sat by the phone, waiting all day for you to call.

Calling again on the knowledge of Virginia Satir, "the more one values oneself, the less one demands from others."[8] Parents who are without self-esteem and also not grown up always seem to need more and more. Constantly dissatisfied with their children's efforts to please, they never get enough attention, love, time, pleasure, credit, praise, or reward. Unlike mature parents who thrive on doing as much as they can for themselves as long as possible, "ungrown-up" parents without self-esteem want everything done for them—and by their children. Although in *Your Best Is Good Enough* I called them "difficult parents" and devoted an entire chapter to exploring their nature, I now dub them simply as "ungrown up." The newer, more basic title does not in any way dilute the menace they pose to their well-intentioned, exasperated children. As parents who appear to have made an art out of continuous, self-serving harassment, "they can be intimidating in the force with which they inflict their demands; demeaning in their criticisms of sincere filial support."[9]

Naturally, because these parents demand more than their children or anyone else can realistically give, they cannot trust. Like Sarah, whose story will unfold in Chapter 4, they believe their children do not care about or for them; that they will abandon them in their hour of need. As a result, in a destructive, never-ending cycle, they demand increasing tokens of proof of their children's loyalty, while in the process pushing them further away. Creating the mechanics for a self-fulfilling prophecy, a parent rumbles, How can I trust my son when he doesn't visit often enough and when some days he even forgets to call. How can a son be too busy to call his mother!

As children must revise an earlier, internalized image of their parents as all-powerful, infallible, and unequal to them in worth and status, so must parents develop a new perception of their children. Parents with a healthy dose of self-esteem execute this shift naturally and with grace long before they reach old age. Having raised children to be independent—to live their own unique lives—they have no need to hold on to them as children. These parents not only rejoice in their children's lives but anticipate the richly diverse opportunities friendship with them offers.

Parents who, despite their advanced chronological age, have been unable to navigate this turn in family development whereby their children become their peers, can stir up terrible tempests. Preaching, demanding, manipulating, listing fossilized injustices from yesteryear, intoning sacrifices, and exercising a wide range of other toxic strategies designed to inflict pain and guilt, they tyrannize their children into submission. Desperately needing their children as children so they can retain their parental role and sometimes unconsciously wanting the nurturing from them they never received from their parents or spouses, they drive their children from their lives.

Such parents behave like adolescents and, if they really want healthy emotional connection, they have no choice but to change. If their children can muster enough self-worth to stand up to them as adults who refuse to tolerate their tirades, as Ellen eventually did in the preceding story, they will be forced to see the futility of their childish ways. Those too immature to be responsive to their children's pleas will lose the precious, life-sustaining connection they desire.

Both immature, unwise parents and immature, unwise children have something important in common—they like to blame one another for their own unhappiness. As in marital battles, each points the finger at the other rather than take responsibility for his or her own actions.

A 75-year-old widowed mother, Leah, laments that her life would be happier and lot less lonely if her daughter, Sue, were to call and see her more often. When I suggest to Leah that perhaps she has the inner resources to create her own contentment, she becomes enraged, warning me that I am taking Sue's side. When I also point out to her that in the retirement community where she lives there are many people who would be happy to have her as a friend and that the community's daily activities could bring pleasure to her life, she responds, "What do I need all that for! That's my family's job!"

Refusing to hear my advice, Leah continues to badger Sue with phone calls and, frequently, makes surprise visits to her home or office not only to make Sue feel guilty but with the hope that these childlike tactics will force Sue to comply. After all, Leah incorrectly presumes, this way Sue will see how miserable she is and will realize that she is to blame. Old, but neither wise nor grown up because she is unable to take responsibility for her life, Leah does battle with her daughter, insisting that her daughter's behavior is at the root of her chronic misery.

Is there hope for Leah and Sue? Maybe and maybe not. Leah is physically well, bright, and interested enough in the world around her to read the *New York Times* every day. If she is willing to channel her considerable energy into taking a good look at herself and her self-defeating behavior, there's a good chance to heal this relationship. If Leah continues to blame Sue for her despair, remaining stubbornly entrenched in this position, the answer is an unequivocal "no."

Children usually blame parents for their unhappiness. Consider the hours we spend with the psychotherapist assigning blame to our parents for all they did or did not do to us. In psychotherapy, however, no matter what its particular leaning, treatment usually ends when the client stops blaming his parents and looks inward for the answers that enable him to take charge of his life. At that pivotal point, the client knows he has grown up.

Still, many children live out their days blaming a parent or parents for their position in life. Whether it is unhappiness in marriage, failure at a job, the inability to make friends, eating or drinking too much, or a volatile temperament, a grown child usually will find a way to shove responsibility onto the parent's lap. Our parents made mistakes, but so did their parents. Certainly they hurt us, but they were hurt too. Perhaps we all come from dysfunctional families, but so what! Most of us, I believe, are healthy enough and old enough at this point to accept our parents as they are; to see them as no different from the rest of us—wounded, fallible, and frightened mortals who are doing the best they can to find love and meaning in life. We must realize, too, that as long as we continue to blame them for everything we are or that happens to us, we are not grown up. "Get off the victim-of-my-parents bandwagon" might very well be the thirteenth step of the 12-step recovery programs that have become so popular in America. In the context of this writing, of course, the time to do it, to take responsibility is now, when parents are still alive and we can do some real talking face to face.

Not long ago, a middle-aged close acquaintance told me a funny but unfortunate story about his mother and himself. Knowing that I can never have my fill of stories concerning any facet of a grown child's relationship to a parent, Herb described his rather bizarre relationship with his mother:

> I've never told this to anyone before and I really feel a little ashamed and disloyal to my mother in relating it to you, but what I have to say may help you in your work with others. I am a first-born son with a special and, I know, neurotic relationship to my mother. I've had professional help with it and, although I've been able to change some of the ways I relate to her, I've not had the courage to change this particular pattern.
>
> For as long as I remember, at least from the time I left home to go to college and work, I called my mother every day no matter where or when. My wife (Bobbi) always went along with it, but now we are both approaching 65 and she's getting a little fed up with it. We've started going away to Florida for two months every year, and I really resent calling her from driving stops along the way and when we are there. I know it's crazy because I've been doing it all my life, and now that she's old and warrants this kind of attention, I don't want to give it to her. For the first time, I really feel trapped and almost enslaved by my mother's power. I blame her for the tension between Bobbi and me, because Bobbi says she has finally had enough of all this and wants me to end these phone calls once and for all. I just can't seem to tell my mother how I feel. I am completely miserable because of my mother, and have actually developed an ulcer over this conflict. It's literally eating up my stomach. Every time I call her, my stomach is in knots and then it gets even tighter when I have to face my wife.

That a son blames his 84-year-old mother for his stress and marital difficulties may be a funny and entertaining vignette, but it is not amusing when one considers the tragic results. To be sure, there are piles of history leading to this dysfunctional entwinement, but the point is, Herb is not taking responsibility for his own life. As long as he continues to avoid taking a stand with his mother in hopes of finding a solution, he not only perpetuates the problem and his own guilt but, despite his worldly successes, he remains very much a little boy.

Having enough self-esteem, taking responsibility for your own happiness, demonstrating respect for other people's inner sensibilities, and behaving with appropriate restraint are only the bare bones of growing up. Although they are of great value because they offer concrete guidance, more subtle aspects of human nature wash over the terrain of parent-child relationships during these later years of life. They pertain to loss and disappointment, touching us in our innermost layers, and hold a significant place in our discussion of the meaning of growing up. As concepts, existential yet intrinsic both to the tasks of aging and to the interplay of the generations, they must be examined. A person cannot be considered fully grown up or a whole human being until he or she gives these notions considerable thought and integrates them into life.

Parents and children who want to enjoy mature, harmonious relationships with each other must acknowledge that in the realm of intimate attachments, preconceived notions and agendas often do not work. Much that children and parents plan for simply doesn't happen. It's no one's fault when things go awry, because people, who to begin with are unpredictable, complex, imperfect, and vulnerable, become even more so with people in whom they have an emotional investment.

Few parents escape the pain of unrealized hopes that accompanies the process of raising children. The disappointments, unfulfilled expectations, and shattered dreams bring considerable heartache to daily lives. At times they seem insignificant, as in the following vignette about Sylvia, but they must be taken seriously to understand the consequences they bring.

Sylvia was a 74-year-old mother who spent almost an hour sobbing in my office because her children did not give her and her husband the fiftieth wedding anniversary party she expected. Her story illustrates the deep hurt unfulfilled expectations can cause. The children of all Sylvia's friends had or were planning to have such celebrations for their parents. It seemed she had waited and fantasized about this moment forever, including what she would wear and what kind of speech she would make.

Sylvia could not understand why her children failed to come through for her with this great gesture. "They knew," she told me, "how much this party would mean to me. I would always tell them in great detail about the parties Mike (her husband) and I went to for our friends. My daughter, especially, knew. Why, she and I would discuss what I should wear and sometimes we would shop together for a new dress for me for the occasion. What happened was they took us out to dinner instead: just the two children and four grandchildren. It was in a really expensive restaurant with gourmet food but it wasn't what I wanted. I later—not that night, of course—told them of my disappointment. I told them I was mad! They said they were sorry, but they were just too busy with work and their children's activities to have the energy and time to plan for and give the kind of party I wanted. So, what can I say? I feel they didn't care enough to do this one big thing for me. They said I should be grateful that they celebrated in a swanky restaurant with the immediate family present. They even said this has more meaning than a big shindig with lots of people they don't even know. Well, for me the party would have meant more!"

Some might dismiss Sylvia's disappointment as trivial. But to Sylvia, and this is where it counts, her loss was serious business. Essentially a rite of passage, this party was to mark the supreme moment of her life when her children would prove to her and the world they really cared. Inconsolable, Sylvia not only felt shame before her peers but was experiencing deep feelings of loss. What she had hoped for and dreamed about was not to be. Well into the final years of her life, feeling resentful, angry, betrayed, and unloved, Sylvia was in despair. It was as if the very basis of her existence had collapsed. Her children had disappointed her beyond anything she could have imagined. There was no way she could forgive them for the pain they caused her.

Every parent and child, consciously or unconsciously, creates a set of expectations for how he or she would like the other to be. These expectations form our most cherished hopes and dreams and can even get to the point where they pass beyond fantasy into fixed reality—where perspective becomes impossible, as it did with Sylvia. If unfulfilled, they have the power to devastate the lives, if not the spirit of parents and children.

Depending upon their values, personalities, and backgrounds, parents might hold some of the following expectations for their children: that they marry within their religion and race and have children; that they never get divorced; that they are good students and attend the "right" college; that they form only heterosexual relationships; that they love and get along with their siblings; that they are athletic, thin, good-looking, and perfect in mind and body;

that they choose only certain jobs and make lots of money; and that they live nearby.

So it goes; the list has the potential to be infinite. Believe me, nothing is too inconsequential to be excluded from the litany. Several years ago when I was the social-worker member of a geriatric assessment team, I listened at first incredulously, later compassionately to an 80-year-old man tell me how he could not shake off his hurt over his one and only son giving up what might have been a career in professional baseball. To this day his disappointment burned inside him, making it impossible for him to be close to a son he truly loved but who let him down.

The point is that any one of a number of unrealized, dearly held expectations has the power to sour an elderly parent's remaining days. As with Sylvia or the 80-year-old father, these expectations make a wall between parent and child that at this time in their lives both would like to tear down.

Children, too, carry their own laundry list of expectations. Wishing their parents were more loving, less critical, less self-centered, more nurturing, they may ache with disappointment. Their expectations, coming in the form of questions that ring childlike and desperate, beg serious answers. Why doesn't my father attend his only grandchild's college graduation? Why does my mother have to play bridge instead of baby-sitting for me? Why can't my mother give me credit for all that I've accomplished? Why can't my mother ever be complimentary? Why do my parents continue to give my brother money when it's clear that he will never amount to anything? Why does my father always have to talk about himself instead of inquiring about my family or me? Why can't my parents ever give me a hug or hold my hand?

Parents and children, children and parents, all disappointed: grieving for something wished for and unfulfilled; something expected and not received. Unless parents and children learn that in all significant human relationships loss, imperfection, sorrow, and joy are natural, they are doomed to spend whatever time is left tormenting themselves with thoughts of what could have been. Squandering energy on a past that can't be changed, they only stoke the coals of self-pity, bitterness, and helplessness. It is far better to grieve for parent-child relationships that were not what we hoped and to accept each party for what he or she is. We must move forward into the remaining days resolving to understand and forgive the negatives and to seek out and recognize the positives. None of us is perfect and in all intimate human relationships—but especially parent-child—we inadvertently let each other down sometimes. This is what being grown up is all about. This is the only attitude that can bring some inner contentment and allows compassion for all of us flawed motals, and it is certainly worth integrating into a philosophy for living.

This process of accepting loss and moving on has come to be known as "letting go." Almost a household term because of its frequent use in self-help books, it is, nevertheless, the key to living a serene life.

In his best-selling book, *The Road Less Traveled*, Dr. Scott Peck lists "the major conditions, desires, and attitudes that must be given up (let-go) in the course of a wholly successful lifetime." Included in his list are seven that directly pertain to the theme of growing up: "the dependency of childhood, distorted images of one's parents, authority over one's children, the sexual attractiveness and/or potency of youth, the fantasy of immortality, the independence of physical health, and ultimately, the self and life itself."[10] Representing the essence of letting go, while likewise capturing the full meaning of wisdom, they provide a perfect framework for summarizing this chapter.

First of all, children who persist in seeing their parents through the distorted lenses of childhood are not grown up. As long as they cannot let go of the image they hold of their parents as perfect and powerful people, the goal of maturity is forever out of their reach. Not only do they remain *dependent children*, they cannot be the *dependable adults* their parents need at this time of their lives. (See Chapter 5.)

One of the major themes of this book is Dr. Peck's reference to "authority over one's children." Letting go of the parental power they had over their children is a prime prerequisite for maturity in elderly parents. If parents cannot learn to respect their children as equals rather than as children to be controlled, the closeness they wish to share with them will remain elusive.

Dr. Peck's fourth point applies to parents, old but not wise, who desperately grasp for the sexual attractiveness and vigor of youth.

For them, life in the final years loses all meaning. Ungrown-up, considering the never-never land of the past as the best time of their lives, they miss the opportunities for growth and a new richness in living that only the last part of the life cycle holds.

Although more will be said in Chapter 4 about the treasures of life's second half, the lesson for now is that giving up the sexual attractiveness and/or potency of youth is not easy for most Americans. While accepting old age and death by parents *and* children is essential to developing full maturity, as long as our culture continues to view old age as a problem to be solved or an illness to be cured, the goal is obstructed. When old age is finally acknowledged as a natural stage of life, as the final flow of years to be lived, then Dr. Peck's fourth point will not be considered such a crippling loss. When youth is stripped of its inflated value, giving it up is not so terrible. The act of surrendering it will become what it merely is—preparation for the last lap of life's wonderful journey.

With few exceptions, children who are living in the wake of their parents' old age struggle with Dr. Peck's points about immortality, physical deterioration, and death (see Chapter 3). As I mentioned in Chapter 1, the aging of parents often brings middle-aged adults into full awareness of their own mortality.

As long as parents remain strong and healthy, children in their 40s, 50s, and even 60s believe they, too, will never grow old. It is only when time leaves its mark on their parents' once strong and resilient bodies that children finally must let go of the illusion that they will live forever. It hits them—their parents are aging and dying and so are they!

It is exhilarating to observe what happens to members of my Tuesday-night group when through the filter of a parent's aging, they come to grips with their own finite lives. Experiencing their day-to-day existence on a more conscious level, living in the moment rather than in the past or future, taking nothing for granted, they seem reborn. Life is simultaneously more meaningful and lighter.

Their new awakening brings a degree of appropriate dread as well. Not so much the fear of dying but the "how" of it becomes the spectre with which grown children must finally contend. Suppose I have a stroke like my Dad and have to live out my remaining years in a wheelchair? What if I am ravaged by unrelenting pain from cancer, as my mom was? What if I die all alone? Suppose I end up in a nursing home? What if I develop Alzheimer's, Parkinson's disease, or some other chronic debilitating illness? The questions pour out, and they must if one is to live life consciously as a fully whole and wise person. And sadly, children ponder what they expect from *their* children when *they* reach that certain age.

Of course, as I mentioned in the Introduction, parents and children frequently do not march side by side along the path leading to maturity. One party may take responsibility while the other continues to blame; one may let go of disappointment while the other holds tight; one may be willing to relate as equal, while the other clings to old roles; one may be able to accept the inevitability of old age and death while the other can only deny it; one may have sufficient self-esteem to trust, while the other requires endless, counterproductive demonstrations of love.

Regardless of whether parties are in sync, growing up is always worth the effort. As a journey ending only with death, the process continues for as long as we live. In the context where the days are dwindling parents and children who have been out of step with each other have a special impetus to grow up and finally get it straight. It's now or never.

The journey can be informed, but it is never easy because the road is strewn with all the complex and ambivalent feelings—love, hate, passion, resentment, anger, failure, disappointment—that constitute our emotional lives. With understanding and insight, not only are both parties injured less along the way, but they can actively engage in a healing process where the closeness and love they create while they are alive become memories to sustain and nourish the generations to follow.

3

I Won't Grow Up!

"There is no question that your parents failed you as parents. All parents fail their children, and yours are no exception. No parent is ever adequate for the job of being parent, and there is no way not to fail at it. No parent ever has enough love, enough wisdom, or maturity, or whatever; no parent ever succeeds."[1] The minute I read these pointed, yet stirring words of Chaplin Henry T. Close in *Voices: The Art and Science of Psychotherapy*, I knew they held significant clues to some core questions about what constitutes maturity for children. For until children of this certain age can accept their parents as imperfect people who did the best they could to raise them, they will be unable to forgive their errors and live their own lives as emotionally healthy and happy individuals. Whether the parent can do what is required to grow up is far less important than the child hearing the powerful message of truth revealed in this quote.

There is hardly a Tuesday night when a member of my group does not refer to how a parent's imperfection has in one way or another negatively affected her life. Although she may be in her 50s or 60s and accomplished in significant areas, she will have no trouble summoning up deep-seated anger toward a parent for some wrong or hurt. Even those who usually are prone to listening rather than talking suddenly turn into skillful raconteurs, regaling us with detailed stories about a parent's failure to nurture or perform some parental task. Whether it is intrusion into marital problems, flagrant favoritism toward a sibling, sustained hostility toward a spouse, verbal abuse aimed at inflicting shame, failure to stand up for a child at a crucial time, failure to give necessary praise, insensitivity to a hurt or need, withholding affection, or meting out excessive crticism, there is usually much to tell.

Marcia, the 49-year-old executive director of a social service agency, describes her mother and their relationship:

> As I look back upon my childhood, what I remember most vividly about my mother was her complete fascination with the growth of her long, magenta painted fingernails. Second to her nails came her absorption with her hair and clothes. She played cards and lunched with friends almost every day, and although she did some worthy things for the community where we lived, she was never, ever emotionally involved with my sister, brother, or me. She was never home when we returned from school and she and my dad were out nights a lot attending parties and fund-raising benefits. Believe it or not, I used to wish we were poor, so then my mother would be home more. I envied other children who saw a mother rather than a housekeeper in the kitchen after school. It seemed that all my scholastic and athletic accomplishments were only important as material to brag about me to her friends. I was living proof of what a perfect parent she was. I was an object—her trophy.
>
> In fact, as I recall, and it gives me much pain to say it, but the only praise I ever received from her was always indirect—through others who told me they heard I had the lead in the school play or won the Latin award or whatever, and how proud my parents were of me. My mother went through the correct, stereotypical—right from the movies or television—motions of being the really good, loving mom, but trust me, nothing was there. I'm a social worker, I've read extensively, had professional help—not what you would call an unsophisticated consumer—but I'm still angry and unforgiving. Especially now, when she's approaching 80 and would like a little more from me. Well, I'm angry enough to have nothing to give. She never abused me physically or anything like that. Her abuse was of a more invidious, evil nature; make no mistake, I was damaged nevertheless.

Penny's sketch of her father is no less acrid than Marcia's. Penny is a 55-year-old homemaker whose parents moved in with her and her husband so that she could care for her mother following extensive hip surgery. She vividly relates her experience in this almost four-month period:

> It was devastating for me in the sense that I realized how much I still cannot stand my father, and that I have not been able to accept him as he is. He is the most self-centered human being I know. He doesn't hear a word anyone says; thinks he knows everything about everything; doesn't give anyone a chance to finish a sentence. I feel like a rebellious adolescent when I'm with him, and to think he just spent close to four months with me.
>
> My poor mother! During her entire period of recuperation, he would start each day by asking her how she was, and before she could reply he would tell her all about himself—how he slept, what he ate, the condition of his bowels, what he read or heard on tv, how mad he is at the President. I don't know how she survived all these years with him. Whenever she would attempt to tell him even the slightest bit about her pain or what it was like for her to be so immobilized, he never heard her. When he did hear, he would respond with a shallow, "Oh, you'll be fine, Martha. It's really not that bad, now." Never for a minute did he say, "It must be awful for you; what can I do to help?"
>
> And then when I would help her with her exercises, he would stand there criticizing everything I did. And visits to the doctor! Well, he would contradict every word I said, and we would find ourselves in a hot argument right then and there. At one point he told the doctor he wanted to take Mom home earlier. The doctor was aghast that he could suggest such a thing; that he had no idea how frail Mom was. Not that I personally would have minded, at least if *he* had left, because he almost wrecked my marriage.
>
> He would never give Ed and me a minute alone. He intruded into every conversation; would flick the television channel in the middle of a program to one of his choice. He was no different when we were growing up—requiring constant attention, doing all the talking during dinner, treating Mom like some kind of servant, never, ever doing anything father-like with us or spouse-like with her. And always talking; a constant hum in the background like the sound of the heater in my home. It's all worse now because they need me. I don't mind doing for her; but not for him. But I know I must come to terms with him and the person he is, else I'll be in total remorse when he dies. I must learn to accept him for the self-centered, ridiculous fool he is and forgive him. This is a tall order, I know. But he *is*

my father and I feel it would be very immature of me not to accept some measure of commitment to him in his old age.

Examples abound of what parents did or did not do to or for their children. The extremes of physical or sexual abuse, of course, are the cruelest of parental horrors. Currently much is being written about this subject to help those who have survived. Other forms of neglect or family dysfunction, however, like a parent's workaholism, emotional coldness, or substance abuse also bring deep pain.

With Marcia and Penny, parental self-centeredness was the culprit, although it appeared in different guises. For other people, it might be the polar opposite—a parent's self-sacrifice and over-protectiveness. There is always a hurt or two that a child can recite from the pages of his or her autobiography. Because the hurt is tinged with anger and resentment and most of us do not know what to do with these scary, unacceptable feelings, we either tuck them away or unwittingly take them out on others.

If we choose the former, we repress the feared emotions, pushing them from consciousness. The problem with this kind of adaptation is that they ultimately emerge from hiding in other ominous forms, plaguing us with depression, anxiety, alcoholism, over-eating, and psychosomatic illness. If we opt for the latter, those near and dear to us—spouse, mate, sibling, child, friend—suffer as we relentlessly badger them with rage meant for an earlier cast of family characters. *Displacement* is the psychological term for redirection of painful feelings away from ourselves onto those who have not caused them. Angry at his mother for withholding affection, a husband may "displace" that anger onto his wife, perceiving her as his emotionally cold parent.

To accept a parent as he or she is, human, fallible, and imperfect, and then to forgive, are difficult tasks. Yet, we must, or we are always on the hook, neither free nor grown up. Feeling guilt, shame, or anger, we are forever prone to being manipulated by our parents or to projecting blame onto them for whatever misfortunes life has brought our way. As noted in the previous chapter, if we cannot take responsibility for our own lives, despite gray hair, wrinkles, and perhaps a midlife paunch, we remain always at war with those powerful giants, our parents.

The simple truth of the matter, according to Chaplain Close, is that the process of parenting itself is as prone to holes as Swiss cheese. Since we are human beings rather than robots, mistakes are made. Frequently, it is only when children themselves become parents that the tenuous nature of parenting is finally driven home. Although initially, new parents in a state of enthusiastic innocence swear they will do it better than their parents, they eventually come to the sobering realization that as imperfect people themselves they may do some things better, but they *will* make mistakes. Carefully and painstakingly trying to avoid the errors of their parents, they create their own set of misdemeanors.

When parents in their 50s and 60s acknowledge the sad and stormy times with *their* children, they begin to appreciate the Catch-22 nature of the parenting process. Their newly gained understanding enables them to see their parents in a more compassionate light. No longer judging them quite so harshly, they sigh: "They're only human, and so are we!" Shaking their heads, they marvel how they did it (raised them) in the first place.

What also enables all children—whether or not they are parents—to push away some of the uncertainty and anxiety from these final years with their parents is to understand their parents as people; to see them as the people they were before they became parents. This is not easy, because our parents always "feel" like our parents, but it is nevertheless essential if we are to move forward into adulthood. When I wrote *Your Best Is Good Enough* I devoted an entire chapter, "Seeing Our Parents as People," to the process. In the intervening years, I have come to appreciate even more the significance of this leap for middle-aged children who are struggling to relate to their aged parents in a positive, functional manner.

In his book, *Explorations in Marital and Family Therapy*, James Framo explains what is perhaps the pivotal reason for the resistance of grown children to relinquishing perceptions of their parents as "parents." Says Framo, "One aspect of this anxiety is that when adults relate to parents of today they are, in part, still viewing parents as they did when they were children, when they were small and more vulnerable and when their feelings were experienced in gross categories. When it comes to dealings with parents, the residuals of those early affects of love, hate, shame, and awe almost never disappear."[2] Yet, when parents are old the last thing parents this age need is for their middle-aged children to behave like little children. Needing children to be dependable adults who can guide and assist them in their plans for long-term care, parents by and large, even those as difficult as Penny's or Marcia's, welcome their children's adulthood.

Recognizing our parent's quintessential humanity is a kind of liberation. When we see our parents as fallible people no different from ourselves, we may be surprised at how much more we are able to like them. Even if we discover we do not like them, as Penny did, this is also okay. While Penny's acknowledgment of dislike of her father was hard to swallow, she was proud she had the maturity to do the right thing.

Children who see their parents as people are generally able to summon up compassion for some of their eccentric habits and behaviors. Although we easily overlook our own idiosyncrasies and forgive those of our friends, we do not allow our parents similar grace or generosity. What a pain a parent is because he or she always talks about money, remembers every misdeed done by every relative, refuses to throw away useless articles, or automatically dislikes people who perhaps talk, behave, or dress a certain way. We can spare ourselves lots of aggravation if we sit down with parents to learn a little more about the source of their values and judgments. Barring some unfortunate type of dementia, we may be surprised to find out these strange ways did not spring full blown but have histories that date to childhood. How easy to forget that the mom or dad we see today was once young. Can it be that she actually had a childhood, an adolescence—a youth? Can it be that she went to school, perhaps even played hooky, made her parents mad, went to parties, worried about pimples, and had a boyfriend she was crazy about? How much safer to see a parent as someone who just became who she is, without a past. For this way we can defend against our ever having to grow old. Old age, with its white hair, time-worn skin, arthritic fingers, and cataracts happens just to them, not us.

My experience with my 90-year-old father, Arthur, illustrates how critical it is to see the person behind the parent in this context. Knowing that my father was terrified of his strict father, who rarely spared the rod, and from whom he hid in dread under tables and in closets when he knew he did something wrong, I am able to understand and accept his deep-seated fear of confrontation and what often appears to be his outlandish desire to please everyone. When I juxtapose these psychological dynamics against the unstable social and political climate of his childhood and early adulthood, I can further appreciate his alarmist view of the world as a place where danger lurks around every corner. No wonder he insists I call him the minute I return home after dropping him off at his apartment! No wonder he gave me a cellular telephone for my car for my birthday! No wonder he calls me at least three times the day before his doctor's appointment to make sure I won't forget to pick him up! In his eyes, something bad is always about to happen.

Given a childhood where the disruptions of World War I forced him to spend four months in a freight car traveling to an unknown place that would be home until war's end, his anxieties over long automobile trips and his fears of relocation also make sense. Most elderly like to stay put in their own homes, but my father's fierce desire to be glued to his apartment takes on an added dimension.

It comes as no surprise as well that he lowers his head either in embarrassment or disapproval when I argue with a guest at dinner or that he trembles with fear when he happens to be privy to the scary emotions of a heated family dispute. His reprimands of my impatience, bluntness, and impulsiveness, which at one time drove me into a state of unbridled fury, are no longer construed as personal criticisms. Since I understand how in his view I can be overwhelming, I am able to accept his behavior as natural for who he is: a man who most of the time functions in a state of high anxiety. His fears of loss, calamity, and confrontation, exacerbated by the normal dependencies of old age, had their origin at a much earlier time in his life. This history tells me much about Arthur the person, who is also my aged father. It also tells me a great deal about myself.

Yet, my father and I are separate people. His mother and father were different from mine and so were the experiences that molded his life. He is entitled to his quirks. Had he been able to work things out with *his* father so that he could see him as a person, perhaps today Arthur would be a calmer, more relaxed man.

Of practical importance, since my father is elderly, is that understanding his multiple and chronic anxieties enables me to assess his life needs with objectivity and deal compassionately with his dependencies. I know that if possible, he must remain in his own home until his death; that relocation to a care facility would be devastating for him. I know, too, that as much as my husband and I would like to have him over to dinner every week, he would prefer our dropping meals off to him so that he can remain home. I know that when he is especially anxious, a long phone call or visit makes a difference, for then he needs to talk. I know that when he is anxious he also needs a big, comforting hug.

Knowing my father as a person, understanding what is firmly entrenched in his personality, I know there are certain things about him that will never change. Consequently, rather than nag, I devote energy to those areas where the potential for extra intimacy exists. We enjoy, for example, talking about Russian history, excitedly exchanging bits and pieces of knowledge on everything from Ivan the Terrible to Boris Yeltsin. Since both of us also love Western films, we try at least once each week to watch a *Bonanza* rerun or rent a video. Afterwards, we love to dissect the plot and analyze the characters. It seems there's always someone in the cast who reminds him of a person from his past, now dead. He will then reminisce about that person and other friends he has lost, often steering the conversation into the terrain of death and the meaning of his own life. These moments, deeply personal, are among the best we share.

Some grown children who have learned to understand the source of a parent's annoying ways are able to turn impossible situations into mutually satisfying ones. Alex, immediately comes to mind. Alex's father, Ben, 77 and retired, was at one time the largest distributor of meat in a tri-state area. Taking pride in building his own business from scratch, Ben liked to boast to anyone who would listen that not only did he have every good restaurant as a client but that he had eaten in all of them as well. As a result, he believed his word was the final one on which were superior in service and cuisine. Forgetful at times, and without a trace of modesty over considering himself the arbiter of good dining, Ben would repeat ad nauseum the same stories about what and where he ate. Alex, impatient with his father's out-of-date assessments, competitive, and equally opinionated, only wanted to argue with him to prove him wrong. Their debates, as Alex described them to me, were bitter and destructive. Eventually realizing how childlike he was, Alex related the following:

I finally see what a colossal jerk I was that I had to play a game of "one-up" with my dad. At his age, he has a right to be proud of a business that he built all by himself. Especially so since my grandfather told him he didn't have the brains or gumption to do it. Now that I've stopped rebelling like some kind of teenager, I really am able to have a good time with him. I don't have to win or be a big shot anymore. In fact, I feel much better about myself, now that I'm grown up enough to sit back and let him have his say. It makes me feel great to know that I have the power to make my dad happy; to give him such a gift.

Alex has, indeed, given his father a gift, a precious one born of a grown son's ability to see his parent not as a tyrant to overthrow but as a human being with a deep need to be valued for his particular knowledge and material success. In what seems a small gesture, permitting his father to be king of the territory, so to speak, Alex not only gave Ben recognition and love, but in so doing, he also reached a new level of maturity.

A visit to the South Boston neighborhood where her Irish mother spent the first 25 years of her life helped Maggie to understand the wounded woman that lay behind her mother's punitive parental mask. Maggie had always believed that her mother's anger was directed at her and, as a result, wasted futile hours and days trying to placate her. Eventually, she was able to see it was time to give up the battle. "I know it all now," she sighed in resignation.

I know where my mother's fury comes from. Seeing that street where her house and the houses of her aunts, uncles, and cousins still stand, I know why she didn't want to leave Boston after she married my father. She was enveloped in love and security all the time. It must have been quite wonderful for her, always having someone to be with, to talk to, to have a cup of tea with, to run to when things were rough in her own home. I wouldn't have wanted to go to New Jersey either, to live in my husband's strange land with his strange family. No wonder she's always bitter and always talking about how things have never been the same for her since she left her family. She just cannot let go of her old life. I see, too, why my father and she had to separate. That little trip gave me real insight into her personality. I used to think I was the one who was responsible for that fire in her belly—that I had done something to displease her, that she was angry and despised me. Now that she is old and I am the one, out of my four siblings, to care for her, it is important that I understand all that made her into who she is. I know that I cannot change her, nor do I have a right to. Believe me, I am kinder to her and have forgiven her her many emotional abuses of me.

If children cannot see their parents as people during this later period when they are grown and their parents are aged, they run the risk of being seriously stressed. As I mentioned in Chapter 1, this is the time when parents turn to children for assistance with some of their dependencies. It is also the time when grown children want to live. The tension produced by this conflict is inexorable. If children have not sufficiently separated from their parents to see them as people, those who feel responsible for their total welfare or who cannot say "no" for fear of parental reprisal will burn out as caregivers. Governed by guilt rather than reality, they are unable to set healthy limits on what they can and cannot do for a parent.

Children, on the other hand, who see their parents as imperfect, vulnerable human beings can forgive them, discover ways to encourage intimacy with them, and live their own lives free of crippling guilt. As caregivers, and as equals and partners, they assist their parents in making appropriate decisions for their care. Seeing parents as they are rather than through filters clouded with earlier neurotic impressions, they are able to evaluate their needs with objectivity and gentleness. "Had I only taken the time to talk with the old man sooner, I would have saved myself a lot of grief." Joe explained about finding a bit of crucial information about his 79-year old dad. "I would have learned that he lived as a bachelor for seven years before marrying my mom—that he could make stew and soup, sew buttons on his shirts, do his laundry, and even iron. I would have known he was able to do more than I figured he could after she died. My wife, brother, and I worried ourselves sick over how he would manage as a widower. In fact, I wouldn't have given a nickle that he would make it for a year without her. See, Mom did everything for him, so we ran ourselves crazy doing the same thing. He hated our taking over the way we did. We took away a lot of his independence. After awhile though, I stopped with some of the running and began to hear him instead. I learned about his remarkable survival skills. We all had done him a great disservice."

Children who are of that certain age *and* mature must also acknowledge that the person behind the parent is elderly. Such acknowledgment requires more than intellectual awareness of a parent's forgetfulness, increased ramblings, or loss of vision or hearing. More than recognition of a parent's chronological age— Oh God, my mother is 86!—it is a willingness to accept at your deepest level that a parent is no longer able to be the haven of emotional and physical support he or she once was. We realize a reversal has occurred and our parent needs us much more than we need him or her. This is not a reversal in role, for parents are always parents, but a reinforcement of emotional dependability. More than help with chores like marketing or balancing a check book, parents need to know their children are there for them during the darker hours, when loneliness, depression, illness, and uncertainty invade their lives.

Fully facing a parent's old age with its accompanying losses means, essentially, we must be there for them as grown-up children—reliable, trustworthy, resourceful, and inwardly strong. This adult "being there" requires that we directly confront our own ultimate mortality with the poignant recognition that we are each other. Acknowledging this does not mean children have to live their parents' old age for them. No one can do that for anyone. Old age is a road each and every one of us, if we're lucky enough, must travel alone. Part of growing up is the pain of realizing that we cannot cross this border into our parents' world. We cannot, as much as we would like, absorb all the hurts, losses, and grief that constitute their daily existence. We cannot make the pain go away. Consequently, we must accept a kind of sad alienation from their lives.

Recognition of my own unwillingness to grow up and of my inability to accept a parent's old age, with its scary intimations of mortality, hit me with a zing one noontime when I entered my parents' apartment, taking for granted that the weekly lunch I had eaten there for several years would be waiting. Although the table was set and the breadplate full, my mother, pale and shaken, could do no more. Leaning for support against the sink where the salad fixings lay untouched, my mother looked as if she were about to topple over.

Eating with my parents on my day off was a special weekly routine. I would walk through the door, leave all my cares behind, and in the security of their house sit down and be served a delicious meal by my mother. For a few hours every week I could be a girl again, with a mother young and strong enough to dote and wait upon me. Indeed, my mother never sat down until she saw that my plate was full and there was nothing further she could do to please me. My mother's greatest joy was feeding her family, symbolic not only of how much she loved us but the means by which she felt her most whole and realized self. Seven years after her death, whenever I enter what is now my father's apartment, I still smell the sweet aroma of her cooking, compelling me to come to grips again with just how much I miss all her nurturing ways.

Although in *Your Best Is Good Enough*, I wrote about this episode as one where I felt rage at my mother for not being able to express her love for me any more in this meaningful way, I am now able to view it from yet another perspective. Sure, I was angry with her then for, of all things, letting me down by growing old, but I now understand that something else was percolating on a deeper level. With more than a little shame I confess that for years before that lunch, I was living in a state of complete denial over her aging, refusing to see how infirm and frail she had become.

My mother was 83. She had been diagnosed with Parkinson's Disease five years earlier and also suffered from osteoporosis and painful arthritis in her hips and legs—all clear signs of advancing old age, to be sure. On an intellectual level I was aware of these dramatic physical changes—after all, I was the one who took her to doctors' appointments, and as a clinical social worker, would discuss with them the course of her illnesses. But on a deeper, emotional level they never registered.

It was obvious to me then that I had not grown up, nor did I want to. Refusing to recognize that my mother now needed me as an adult, I preferred to languish under the illusion that as long as she could still cook for me she would always be the mother she was and I her little girl.

On that day when there was no lunch waiting for me, I was abruptly hurled into maturity. My life was laid out in front of me just as clearly as my mother's marvelous food used to be spread out on her kitchen table. My mother was old and I was helpless to change this reality; she needed me as she never had; I wanted to care, with love, for her as best I could; I would grow old; she was me; I would need my children; I would die.

A 56-year-old daughter, Roseanne, whom I saw in counseling for two years, also could not accept that her 80-year-old mother, who lived around the corner from her, was old. Roseanne's mother, Marie, had been emotionally available to Roseanne throughout her troubled life. Marie, wise, strong, and positive in attitude, was at Roseanne's side through a difficult divorce and helped nurse her chronically ill grandchild (Roseanne's daughter). When Marie became frail and debilitated, Roseanne could not acknowledge her decline with its concommitant physical and psychological limitations. She continued to ask Marie for help with certain household chores and to be an ear for her unending personal woes and complaints. Because Roseanne had been dependent upon Marie all her life, she could not bear to see her as less than what she once was. She still needed her as rock and support.

Only when Roseanne was able to stop denying her mother's infirmities would she understand how immature she had been. Fortunately, in Roseanne's case, Marie, who had always been there for her daughter, did not let her down. Infinitely wise and grown up herself, she continually reminded Roseanne that, "I'm an old and sick woman and I cannot take care of you any more. I won't be around forever, you know, and it's time you learned to take care of yourself!"

Though Roseanne did not want to hear, Marie fought tenaciously to get her message through. When the words finally penetrated and Roseanne was able to acknowledge the loss of her mother as her mainstay, she excitedly told me the following:

> For the first time in my life, I feel really strong and independent. I feel grown up. It feels good to be able to give and do for Mom. All those years that I thought Mom and I were close, there was something missing. She was doing everything for me, taking care of me, and I was giving nothing back. I was taking all the time; it was a one-way relationship—kind of like a baby nursing at her mother's breast. Now everything is different. I've changed, and our relationship is closer. I'm the capable, adult person I had it within myself to be. And I'm 57—just goes to show that people can change, no matter how old they are.

While acceptance of our parents' aging is one of the most difficult developmental tasks, it becomes extra hard in a society where
longevity is ever on the rise. Scientists, in fact, tell us that by the
year 2080, the average life span for men will be 94 and for women,
100.[3] Although we have not yet arrived at this dubious pinnacle, 1
out of 10 children in their late 60s and 70s has a surviving parent.
For such children, the belief that they and their parents are immor-
tal is easy to imagine. A colleague speaks of how this phenomenon
surfaces in the nursing home where she is director of social services:

> Some children have lived their whole lives with a parent always
> on the scene. It is really quite beyond their ken to imagine life with-
> out him or her. And if they have not reached a certain level of matu-
> rity, and sometimes even if they have, they are terrified they won't
> survive without parental structure. What typically happens in the
> nursing home is that these children refuse to accept a parent's natur-
> al decline. They say things like, How come my mother can't play
> Bingo or do arts and crafts this year when last year she did those
> activities? They don't recognize that the human life cycle is finite.
> That no matter what medical science can offer, their parent is ulti-
> mately going to die. Sometimes they expect the impossible from us,
> telling us we are not doing enough. But we cannot stem the natural
> passing of the years with their accompanying decline. We cannot
> take their parents back to where they were a year ago. Of course, at
> bottom, given the advancing age of these children and their own ill-
> nesses and arthritic aches, the real problem is acceptance of their
> own mortality.

Peter Pan, in the Broadway musical of the same name, sings, "I
won't grow up . . . I'll never grow-up. . . . 'cause growing up is
awfuller than all the awful things that ever were."[4] Certainly, to
remain a child forever would be a delightfully carefree experience.
Without responsibilities and worries, like Peter, we could fly
through and over life as incredibly light in mood and spirit as only
a child can be. Unlike Peter, however, we just might have parents.
But, of course, in Never-Never Land they would not grow old,
would always serve us lunch, would always be our rock and support, and eternally interested in our latest moans and groans.

This state of affairs sounds easy and quite wonderful. Yet when
we give the matter extra thought, we realize not only is this fanta-

sy, but that such a life is without richness. Lacking disappointment, pain, challenge, or responsibility to anyone but ourselves, existence would be a bland, colorless mixture of perennial good times, fun, and merriment. It would be fine for a while, to be sure, like a holiday or a vacation, but not for the long run. Ultimately, it is life without meaning, a life in which the players are spiritually empty. Certainly Wendy realized the sterility of this existence, or else she would have stayed with Peter.

Growing up is about responsibility—first, for ourselves and our lives; second, for those whom we love and their lives, which, within realistic limits, includes our parents. With responsibility, however, comes unavoidable pain, the pain of making decisions, of acknowledging loss of control, of accepting failure, of facing helplessness and disappointment. Growing up means, as Peter continues to sing, to be prepared "to shoulder burdens with a worried air" and sometimes to wear "a serious expression in the middle of July." Children of this certain age who are mature and wish to be dependable for their parents are forced to live with the angst wrought by these sober limitations.

Growing up is also about having respect for our emotional and physical limits. Tied to the concept of self-esteem, maturity is knowing what we can or cannot do without hurting ourselves in some way. The moral dictate that children must care for their aging parents the same way their parents cared for them in infancy and childhood makes it hard for many children to deal with unrealistic expectations of what they would like to do for their parents. Thinking anything short of this type of complete commitment is abandonment, they insist on doing it all, giving back in kind what was given to them early on. The old expression that "one mother can take care of 10 children, and 10 children cannot take care of one mother," is still very much alive in our culture. The notion that when our parents age they become children to be cared for also powerfully colors children's expectations.

Should these misleading myths not be enough, their parents' own demands for restitution add the finishing wrappings to their already heavy package of guilt. When counseling these children, I find them unable to hear me. No matter how I try to explain that the model of total care does not apply, they argue that if their parents did it for *their* parents, so must they.

The point is, unlike childcare, parent care is not a natural stage of life. Elaine M. Brody, senior research consultant for the Philadelphia Geriatric Center and a foremost authority on caregiving children, sums up this dilemma in these words: "We're all genetically programmed to go through certain psychological and biological stages in life, but we're not programmed to take care of a parent. Having to take care of a parent can happen at any time in your life. I've known 80-year-old caregivers taking care of 100-year-old parents." Besides, she continues, ". . . it's quite different when a young mother has the stamina and strength to take care of a relative than when a 70-year-old woman is taking care of a 90-year-old mother."[5]

From yet another perspective, the notion of parent care as the norm can seem almost absurd. If it were a natural stage, when or where would we ever get some kind of break from the drudgery of raising a family and work itself? There would be nothing to look forward to; "our turn" would simply never arrive as we jump from rearing children to caring for parents. I can envision crowds of grown children taking a deep breath, and that's about all, in preparing to leap into the last frontier of parent care. Meanwhile, *their* children brace themselves for a similar ascent (or descent) in the not-too-distant future.

Aside from unrealistic parental expectations, the problem of role reversal, and the harmful attitude of the "mother-ten-children" slogan, the Commandment "Honor thy Mother and Father" seems to ask for so much. Rather than lighten the load for grown children or clarify expectations, its broad message only creates more confusion and guilt. The problem is not in the Commandment itself, which will be viable as long as there are parents and children, but rather in the interpretation of the process of "honoring" as it applies in our current times. In other words, the challenge is not in the "why" of the Commandment but the "how" of it. How can the command to honor your father and mother be made to work in a world so different from when Moses received the tablets from God? How can it be revised to help children understand that to "honor" a parent does not mean returning total care?

Of course, every family is unique in what its members can or can't do for their elderly parents. Some grown children manage total responsibility for their parents' care without stress. Their parents move in with them, they care for their physical and emotional needs, and they are their parents' mainstays and support. The care they offer until a parent dies is superb in both quality and quantity, and these children and their parents deserve admiration and recognition. From my clinical experience, however, they represent a small minority. Most children who live with their elderly parents, and about whom Dr. Vivian Carlin and I wrote in our book, *Should Mom Live with Us*, find their lives considerably strained. As Dr. Carlin and I point out, unless a parent has ample physical privacy and there are substantial finances to arrange for respite and home health services, caregiving children and their families experience a wide range of personal, marital, and family upheaval.[6]

Even when parent and child do not live together—the more common scenario—the pull of the Fifth Commandment is strong. The caregiving son or daughter, under unrelenting moral pressure to be the good child who honors his or her parent, feels tension. Working and tending to her own family while shopping, marketing, and cooking for Mom, a daughter always feels she should be doing more. She even questions, for example, whether she has a right to leave Mom for a much-needed vacation for herself.

Even the son or daughter who lives thousands of miles away from an elderly parent and, consequently, is limited in what he or she can do is still torn with guilt and despair. Carla, a 53-year-old daughter, relates how it is for her:

> It hurts. I'm helpless. I want to be there for my mother the way she wants and the way I know I *should* be, but I cannot. I am divorced, have my own consulting business, a handicapped daughter and, to top it off, live 1,500 miles from her and my father. Every time she calls, she tells me how tired she is; that she knows she ought to see the doctor, but is waiting for my next visit so that I can go with her; that my father, who was no different in the past, is not helping her now; that they are having terrible marital problems. So what else is new, I ask myself! She pushes all my guilt buttons. I start to feel the clutch in my stomach. My impulse is to leave my job, my daughter, and to jump on the first plane to be with them—to rescue them. Then I can prove to her that I am a good daughter, after all. Most of the time I walk around believing I'm a bad one.

There is a clear and present danger to parents whose children are driven to return total care. This danger is generally overlooked because we tend to view excessive caregiving only in terms of its stressful effect upon the daughter or son. It has to do with effectively turning our parents into infants. By doing everything for parents, children take away whatever control their parents have left. Solicitous and overprotective, they do their parents a cruel disservice by killing them with kindness, thereby robbing them of those precious ingredients that form the core of their self-worth. Often, they may go so far as to speak for them, finish their sentences, and to make decisions for them that they are perfectly capable of making themselves.

I remember a mother who roughly pushed away her daughter as she attempted to help her button her coat. The mother, uncommonly regal and poised in her wheelchair, stridently reminded her that although her stroke-damaged legs didn't work, her hands were just fine. When I later visited the daughter's home where the mother lived, I was not surprised to find a sullen and withdrawn mother whose life no longer had purpose because her daughter did everything for her. Not even allowing Mother to wheel over to the refrigerator to get and pour juice for herself, the daughter's behavior sapped her mother's spirit to fight back. The flash of life that shone so brightly for that brief moment in my office was gone. Unintentionally, her daughter had robbed her mother of dignity and purpose.

During a workshop for children who take care of or are otherwise involved with their aging parents, a well-dressed and well-spoken banker asked if I had any suggestions about how to make his 86-year-old mother more "cooperative and reasonable." It seemed she rejected his offers to buy her a Medic-Alert disc to wear around her neck, to manage her check book and investments, and to hire someone to come in to do the cooking. Although his mother had recently fallen and seemed more frail, she insisted upon making no changes whatsoever in her life style. The son was at wit's end over his mother obstinacy, wringing his hands in desperation as he spoke. Before I had a chance to counsel him, several other workshop participants shouted almost in unison, "Leave her alone, for God's sake! She's not a child!"

Indeed, she is not a child. At 86 and in full command of her mental faculties, she knows better than anyone how she wishes to live and the risks involved in her choices. Urging her son to respect these choices, I suggested that he do the following: outline what resources for help are available; let her know that if she wishes to take advantage of them, he is there to help; then drop the subject, talking instead about something that will bring both mutual delight. Time is simply too short to waste on issues that create distance rather than meaningful connection.

Daughters and sons who are grown up know that roles do not reverse when their parents become dependent. Although they do see their parents as people, their interactions with them carry a certain reverence. Notice, for example, the way a mature middle-aged child helps her elderly parent cross the street or the way another listens to his parent's concern about something. There is not a trace of condescension in the demeanor of those children. Respect, forged by the parent-child bond and the long history they share, pervades the space between them. No matter how physically or mentally infirm a parent may be, a fully mature child is almost deferential. There is simply no way to avoid the fact that our parents remain our parents, no matter what.

Consider my good friend, Dolores, whose 85-year-old Alzheimer's-stricken mother has not recognized her, her brother, or anyone close to her in more than six years. Dolores still regards her mother as mother, even though she lies in a nursing home day after day, unable to feed herself, walk, or speak, with tubes leading from her body. Knowing how much her mother liked to look attractive in her healthier days, she still talks to her about clothing choices respectfully: "Mom, I bought you these these new nightgowns. They have lace necks, and the colors are your favorites, mauve and pink. I hope you will like them." All communication is in the language of "I" and "you," acknowledging her mother as a separate, autonomous individual, despite her complete lack of control over her life. That horrid "we" or similar baby-talk frequently used by grown children and professionals when addressing the elderly is conspicuously absent, thankfully.

Role reversal, used accurately and accordingly practiced, refers to the turning point in the family when grown children become *dependable* caregiving grown chidren to their parents. It does not mean that children become their parents' parents. To be dependable means to be there as adults for our parents when they need us—not only for that ride to the doctor or to the market but for the emotional goodies of affection, warmth, and moral support. As long as parents are mentally able, we must respect their right to self determination of their needs and how they wish to manage them. And even when a parent is demented, like Dolores' mother, there is a certain boundary that must never be crossed.

Some grown children become responsible for a parent's wellbeing long before they reach their later years. Speak to these children and they will tell you without a minute's hesitation that they have been taking care of a parent or parents for as long as they can remember. They will tell you that they were never children, just little adults dressed in children's clothing. Although frequently coming from families where a parent is an alcoholic or suffers from mental or emotional troubles, they may also orginate in less-dysfunctional families where a parent is simply immature. At an early age, these children learn they must be the ones to rescue, comfort, cover up family secrets and shame, get everyone in the family to like and understand each other, and generally hold the family together. They perform a variety of tasks—cooking and doing household chores, screening phone calls, taking care of their brothers and sisters, and giving the family self-esteem through their achievements. These children are swept away in a storm of what is known today as "co-dependency," which not only eats up their own identitities but also with time becomes a firmly entrenched pattern that resists change. In her brilliant book, *The Drama of the Gifted Child*, Alice Miller describes them as children who in obsessively accommodating their parents' needs while appearing to be perfect, negate their own needs and authentic instincts. Creating a "false self" to please others, they are prevented from becoming whole human beings.[7]

Family therapists have another term for such children; they are called "parental children." Although the "parental child" syndrome may cause problems "if the delegation of authority is not explicit or if the parents abdicate, leaving the child to become the main source of guidance, control, and decisions, it can function well." Such children develop competence and responsibility that serves them admirably throughout life. Receiving approval and praise from a parent, he or she may be the favored child in the family who arrives at adulthood with a sense of mastery, confidence, and capability. Many of these parental children, overly responsible and self-disciplined as a result of their early training, achieve great success later in life. A role that encompasses such positive gains is hard to surrender.

Sherri, 45, typifies the parental child who is satisfied with her place in the family system. Now an architect and community leader, she recounts with a certain amount of pride the events that lead her to her parental role:

> From an early age on, I took care of my mom, so what I'm doing now represents no great change for me. My younger sister and brother were never in the picture in this way.
>
> By at least age 10, whenever I heard Mom crying in her bedroom because of headaches, I would always bring her a cup of tea and hold her hand. My father, who ran a successful paint-manufacturing business, was completely tied to his work. If ever there was a workaholic, it was he. I can tell you my mother never had to worry about a mistress, because his mistress was his business. Anyway, it was customary for him to remain in his office until the wee hours of the morning, often disappointing my mother by not showing up for pre-arranged social engagements. When he stood Mom up, I would play cards with her or we would watch tv together. On these occassions I often went into the kitchen to bake cookies for her. Since I was a pretty exceptional student and not terribly interested in dating, I could give her lots of attention. Besides, it was rewarding to be so special. My mother always told me how wonderful I was, that no daughter was better than I.
>
> Although I am now married with children of my own, I still speak with her at least twice per day and love to send her cards, notes, and little gifts. I am even her personal shopper, for no one knows her tastes better than I. And to this day, I continue to give my father hell for not being more attentive to her. Although what I do takes a lot of energy, I take deep satisfaction in knowing that had it not been for me maybe my parents wouldn't be together today. Or maybe I prevented my mother from going into a psychiatric hospital. I have made a difference in my parents' lives and I consider that a great personal accomplishment. I doubt that I can ever be different.

When parental children are middle-aged and are called upon to take care of their elderly parents, most, unlike Sherri, may for the first time experience tension in their prized role. Taking care of parents while at the same time being responsible to their own families and job is usually more than they can adequately handle.

The case of Julia, a 57-year-old advertising executive who recently remarried, comes to mind. Having cared for her depressed and alcoholic mother for as long as she can remember, she is now angry over her mother's intrusions into her new life. Torn between her own needs for happiness and her 81-year-old mother's need for the level of attention she has become accustomed to, Julia feels guilty and helpless. She believes she can't drop her caregiving role even though her second marriage is jeopardized by her mother's demands. Smart enough to know that her conflict is deep-seated and potentially destructive to her and her marital happiness, she comes to my office for help. The work she has to do is long and painful, requiring courage she thought she did not have. After all, Julia is 57 and has been her mother's parent for most of her life. Consequently, every time she takes a step forward to healthy separation, her mother's powerfully manipulative cries of Help, you're abandoning me! hurl her two steps backward into the old clutch. Eventually, however, Julia asserts her right to live life in accordance with her own needs and takes stock of what she can realistically do for Mother. Releasing herself from the heavy load of the child-parent, she is not only personally free, but feels like a real adult for the first time.

At this point, I hasten to add that most parents do not want their children to give care beyond what they can physically and emotionally manage. They do not want their children to become ill while caring for them; nor do they wish to receive care that springs from guilt and anger. Offering care from emotional depletion is not what honoring our parents is about. Mature, caring parents want their children to thrive—to have it better than they did. Middle-aged themselves not too long ago, they appreciate the shortness of this stage in life and want their children to savor every minute of it.

So, who are the grown-up children? First and foremost, they're the ones who have been able to let go of unrealistic expectations that demand they be all and do all for their parents. They realize that they can meet some of their parents' needs without distress, but they also know that other needs are beyond their capacity to satisfy. They know, for example, they can't fill the emptiness in their parents' lives that results from the death of cherished friends and relatives. They also know they can be available for emotional support, but they can't be a constant companion and entertainer.

Seeing their parents as people, grown-up children realize that some of their character traits always will resist change. The 79-year-old father of one my friends, never one to find pleasure in social activities—in fact, a real lone wolf—will not suddenly become a devotee of weekly bingo games, church suppers, and trips to Atlantic City. No matter how hard my friend tries to persuade him to join the local Golden Age Club, he remains immovable. My friend must accept his father as he is, allowing him to live life on his own terms. And sadly, my own anxious father will always be anxious. I must accept him as he is.

Children who are grown up put sensible limits on their caregiving so they have enough energy left over to be loving when they're with them. Such care, governed by reality instead of primitive nudges from childhood, is unstrained and feels right. Because it is care given from a full heart, the parent is secure in feeling that she will not be abandoned. She trusts her grown child. She sees in her eyes, hears in her voice, feels in her touch that her child is a dependable, mature adult who will not let her down. That parent knows in the deepest layers of her being that she is cared about at all times, including those days when her child doesn't call or cannot visit. It is this internalized emotional knowledge that sustains her and all parents throughout their old age.

Ultimately, grown-up children are able to accept themselves as composits of both the dark and light sides of their parents. Free to acknowledge the dark aspects, they also can credit their parents with the special strengths and gifts they have passed on to them. They do not split off these bad parts, realizing that accepting them is essential to becoming whole people. "Although I have my father's explosive temper and can blame him for this negative piece of my personality, I also have his biting wit and generosity of spirit," says Valerie, 51, who has not only just forgiven her father some of his faults, but in realizing that he is an okay person, affirms that she is too.

Whoever said growing up was easy! Just when we though we had our relationship with our parents all figured out, they are elderly and enter our lives spinning a web of unimagined confusion and disorder. We thought we had accepted and forgiven them their past assaults on our self-esteem and are surprised to learn that some of their misdeeds still bother us. And if we have not accepted or forgiven them, we discover that we now wish for a more wholesome way of being with them. If we mistakenly believe that we could never be as intensely involved with them as when we were children, we are shocked by the frequency and compelling nature of our new interactions with them. We feel smug about the clarity of our loyalties and are astounded by how jumbled and obscure they have become. Torn between the needs of parent and spouse and our own children, we beg to know who comes first. We are pelted with more questions than answers at a time when we need direction. Is it morally okay to lunch with my wife when my mother wants me to spend my day off visiting her? Am I "bad" to prefer playing golf to taking my dad shopping? Should I put off seeing my grandchildren so that I can visit my father? Suddenly we feel as helpless little children. Lost not in Never-Never Land but in a real world where parents grow old and need us, we try as lovingly as we can to balance our obligations to them with those to ourselves.

I doubt there is a finishing line where a person can take a deep breath and say, I've made it; I'm grown up! As long as we are open to life, we are always in a state of becoming. The process is endless. If we want, no matter what age we are, we can grow and grow up, always, however, aware there is more to learn about ourselves and those we love. We have it within us to be all we can be, and that is life's most glorious gift.

For many children, though, growing up is made more difficult by parents, ungrown-up themselves, who define parenthood as perennial power rather than perennial love. The next chapter will explore who these parents are and what they must finally do to get it right. Children, nevertheless, must go forward, even if their parents choose not to. To wait 'til their parents grow up is, after all, a most ungrown-up thing to do.

4

A Parent for All Seasons

The good news for parents is that children *do* care about them in their old age. The bad news is that parents believe otherwise. Although the evidence unequivocably shows that children currently care for their elderly parents to an extent unprecedented in history, this disparity between reality and perception persists. The notion that children do not care is deeply enough entrenched in society to have achieved the status of an actual syndrome. Gerontologists, as early as 1977, named this syndrome the "myth of uninvolvement."[1] Fifteen years later, despite increased public awareness of the efforts of grown children to care for their elderly parents, the myth, with the stronger noun "abandonment" replacing "uninvolvement," persists.[2]

What remains perplexing is how children as well as parents buy into the myth, preferring to believe that somehow they are neglecting their elderly parents. Children who are unquestionably devoted to the care and welfare of their elderly parents have told me not only that they should be doing more, but that they think that in this country children generally dump elderly parents into the cold, bare rooms of institutions. Noted gerontologist Ethel Shanas aptly compared the myth to the many-headed snake from Greek mythology known as the Hydra of Lerna.[3] Like this mythical beast that would grow two heads when one was cut off, the myth of abandonment seems to thrive on each piece of indisputable evidence that disproves its essential premise. What feeds the myth?

Elaine Brody, quoted from an article in the magazine *Psychology Today*, gives us what I believe is the most sensible reason for the myth's indestructibility. Says Brody: "The myth does not die, because at its heart is a fundamental truth. At some level members of all generations expect that the devotion and care given by the young parent to the infant and child should be repaid in kind when the parent, now old, becomes dependent."[4] Because devotion and care of this type is impossible to return, those parents who adhere to the idea of return as an almost universal law of nature find themselves not only angry and disappointed but, indeed, feeling abandoned.

After a recent talk I gave at a senior center, I was approached by Mr. and Mrs. B, a friendly, talkative couple in their middle 70s who were perplexed and dismayed over the present state of affairs between grown children and elderly parents. Their genuine concern over what they perceived as lack of commitment by their own children accurately reflected the prevailing attitude of many parents. Believing that children do not care for their parents as they did in previous generations, they asked in the most forlorn and anguished tone why things were not the same as when their parents were alive. Mrs. B said:

> My mother lived around the corner from us. We saw each other a lot and spent time together. When she couldn't manage on her own anymore, we took her into our home. She lived with us until she one day dropped over dead at the kitchen table. My children were in their late teens when she died so they knew how much we did for their grandmother. They knew how much I cared and how much I loved her. I don't feel that same interest and devotion coming from my son or daughter. I don't think they learned a thing from our example. We feel betrayed by them.

I was taken with their need to talk and their grief over the loss of what they dreamed their relationship with their grown children might be. Hoping I could somehow ease their pain with some supportive words and guidance, I asked them to spell out in more detail their present life situation. I wanted a more complete picture of their children and their relationship to them.

The facts that came to light from our conversation revealed that their children *do* care, that Mr. and Mrs. B are unable to acknowledge that care, and that their expectations of what their children should do for them are based on standards that are far removed from the modern world.

Though it was different from how Mr. and Mrs. B cared for their parents, it was immediately apparent that their son and daughter were deeply committed to their parents' welfare. Their son, who lives three hours away by plane, calls at least once a week, sends videotapes of grandchildren, and visits for a day or two whenever business brings him into his parents' area. Were Mr. and Mrs. B pleased with his efforts to maintain contact? Well, yes, but. . . .

Their daughter, on the other hand, a single parent who lives about 20 miles from them and has a full-time job while raising two adolescent children, still manages to have her parents over to dinner and enjoys shopping excursions with her mother whenever possible. Were Mr. and Mrs. B pleased with her efforts to demonstrate devotion? Well, of course, but. . . .

Despite the compelling evidence indicating their children's involvement and concern, Mr. and Mrs. B continued to believe that something was lacking. Try as I could, I could not get them to verbalize what was bothering them. When I casually suggested that perhaps the elusive ingredient had something to do with their expectations of what they believe grown children owe parents, Mr. B replied, "Of course, I expect them to do what is required." Urging him to explain what he meant by "required," he thought for moment and then said, "You know, to be with us the way we were with our parents. *We* cared for them! They took care of us when we were growing up and when they got old, we took care of them. That's the circle, isn't it? But it doesn't seem to work that way with the younger generation. Don't you agree?"

Mrs. B added, "I know they are busier than we were, especially my daughter who has to raise her children by herself, but that's the point, don't you see. I'm afraid they won't be there for us when we need them."

"What do you mean by that?" I asked Mrs. B. "Well," she responded, do you think either one of our kids would ask us to move in with them? Do you think they would do all that?"

I replied, "I don't know. Perhaps yes and perhaps no. My sense is that somehow you believe that if your children aren't there for you in the exact same way you were for your parents this means they do not care for you at all. Because what I hear is that your children *are there* for you, that they don't ignore you, and that they want to be with you."

Then Mr. B grudgingly said, "I suppose you're right in some respects, *but* something is still missing today in how grown children treat their parents."

Almost palpable, but not quite, I could feel the corrupt presence of the myth of abandonment intrude in our discussion. There it was, raising its ugly head (or heads, to use Shanas' analogy). The facts indicate the opposite situation—that Mr. and Mrs. B's children *do* care and that they are doing the best they can in a variety of creative ways, given the nature of their busy lives, to show genuine concern for their parents. Yet, Mr. and Mrs. B believe their children's efforts fall short. Mr. and Mrs. B feel they did better and more for their parents and they feel abandoned. Where does this distorted perception come from? The myth is doing its divisive work.

You don't have to be a psychologist or expert in family dynamics to understand and empathize with Mr. and Mrs. B. As a 60-year-old parent (and grandparent) myself, under certain conditions I entertain "you owe me" thoughts. Although they surface in a lighter context, they still point up the almost primitive nature of this kind of distorted thinking. In what I can only describe as a knee-jerk reaction, I become hurt and feel a little betrayed when my youngest son, Bruce, 33 and busy in his profession in another city, does not telephone as often as I think he should. I sadly wonder, "Why doesn't he call? Doesn't he know how much I worry about him? After all I did for him, I would think the very least he could do is call me just a bit more often. Is this too much to ask?" Then, of course, all the usual scenes from his infancy, childhood, and adolescence flash before me—endless car pooling, days spent sewing labels in camp clothing, chaperoning school dances, years and years of preparing bag lunches and cooking his favorite pot roast and potatoes. The last scene is always of me teaching him how to park a car. Snickering, because I pompously think that if it weren't for me he never would have passed his driver's test, I finally begin to see how ridiculous I am and pick up the telephone to call him.

Though harmless and funny, this scenario shows how easy it is to slide into the "you owe me" routine. And how can it be otherwise when we, as parents, invest so much of ourselves in our children for so long a period of time? Unlike other species that send their young into the world as soon as they can fend for themselves, we protect and nurture our offspring for well over 20 years in some instances. After all that closeness, is it any wonder that sometimes we think we own our children? Or when they finally leave us, we feel cheated and abandoned? Suddenly, the kids are gone—busy with their families, jobs, friends, and interests, none of which includes us. Once we always knew where they were. Now we never know where they are and what they are doing. Somehow it just doesn't seem fair that after all our hard work, they no longer need us.

Yet, it *is* fair. Loss is one of the things parenthood is about. It is about that unexplainable feeling of emptiness we experience when our children leave our homes to build lives of their own. Parenthood, however, is also about the unique satisfaction we derive from watching our children make it in the world as fully grown up, independent human beings. Knowing they are able to survive on their own, we feel we have succeeded at the major task of parenting. It is in this singularly grand achievement that payback for parents perhaps rests. The "return" to parents, the reward, is their children's success at living. It is not how much care their children can give to them in their old age.

The notion that return lies in endless demonstrations of love and care, nevertheless, holds fast. Besides governing what parents expect, it sticks like glue to the consciences of grown children. Clients I've helped over the years, friends, relatives, and, of course, my Tuesday-nighters punish themselves with thoughts of betrayal and broken vows. "If only I could do more for my mother, after all she did for me and my children," says 48-year-old Theresa with a deep sigh. She goes on to tell me about all the advantages her mother provided at great sacrifice to herself: how she worked at three jobs to send her to a private high school and college, how after her husband was laid off, her mother was there for her with much-needed financial help and baby sitting.

Or, laments Eileen, 56, "I always fully expected that when my parents were old I would be able to pay them back for some of the nice things they did for me. My father's mother lived with us until she died, and in the back of my mind I thought perhaps I would be able to do that for one of my parents. But I can't! My husband has cancer, I must work just to get us by, I do most of the household chores, I have grandchildren I worship and love to be with. I just cannot be with Mom and Dad as much as they would like and the way I know I should." And then through tears, she finishes with, "Oh God, there's no way I ever want my children to feel this terrible pull of obligation and the horrible guilt it creates." Is it any wonder, given this kind of powerful affirmation, that the myth of abandonment endures?

Not so easy to understand, however, is the widespread belief that children took better care of their parents "back then" and that now children dump parents into boarding or nursing homes. With only 6 percent of people over 65 in nursing homes and 90 percent of long-term parent care provided by families, this notion is both absurd and destructive. It is absurd because it flies in the face of solid statistical evidence, destructive because it perpetuates the myth of abandonment. "Back then" or "those good old days" as Elaine Brody refers to them, never existed. How could they, when "back then" people simply did not live that long! Thirteen percent of elderly parents move in with their grown children. When three generations share the same household or live within an hour of one another, they are more likely to live in split-level homes in suburban Philadelphia or Cleveland than in little houses on the prairie. Although the facts show that grown children are out there caring and doing more than ever for their parents, countless Mr. and Mrs. B's *and* their grown children believe the reverse is true.

Times change and so do circumstances. Parents who recognize that rules established for a different era no longer apply have more comfortable relationships with their grown children once they must depend on them for support. Parents who cling to expectations carried over from another time and place, however, feel disappointed, betrayed, and abandoned.

Incessantly reminding their children that they did more and better for their parents, these parents, like Mr. and Mrs. B, are never satisfied with their children's efforts. Something is always missing in their eyes.

Why is it so hard for some parents to understand that the world today is considerably different from the one in which they were raised? The answer does not lie in their ignorance of today's complex society. Most elderly parents with whom I come into contact are avid readers, learners, and tv watchers who often know more about current social, economic, and political forces than their younger counterparts. In fact, many of them who have physical and sensory loss exercise their intellectual gifts as a meaningful way to preserve identity and autonomy. Those whom I counsel and know personally frequently bring me up to date on current events. Many bring me clippings from newspapers or magazines or loan me fascinating books. They are as up-to-date as the talk shows they watch, with an additional insight or two. By and large, they are also keenly aware of developments that directly affect the quality of their lives. From home health care to meals on wheels services, from changes in Medicare laws and Social Security to adult day care and respite programs, those who are able to hear, see, or read generally have an overall good command of what is involved in modern-day parent care.

The answer has to do with something basic to most, if not all, elderly parents. Related to loss, it has to do with their idea of the way parenthood is slipping away and what this loss means to them. When a parent tells a child, "I took care of my mother better than you take care of me," she is dictating to that child as though that child were still little and dependent. Unable to come to terms with her child's adulthood, the parent pushes her obsolete, authoritarian role beyond its usefulness in their current relationship. It is "you owe me" with the added dimension of "I did it more and better with my parent." At its core, of course, is control.

Given the relentless losses—work, health, close friends and relatives, income, and status—that go with aging, it is understandable why a parent might want to grasp at the final bit of control parenthood represents. In the shrinking world of the elderly where there are increasingly fewer ways to express autonomy, control of a parent over a child remains a viable choice. What parents who resort to this are unable to appreciate is that control of this nature is

counterproductive. Alienating children instead of fostering closeness, it creates friction in the parent-child relationship that is frequently self-perpetuating. Simply stated, the more the parent
pushes for control by assuming an authoritarian stance, whether by
"you owe me" or "I did more for my parent," the more the child
pulls away. (Even if a child seems to give in to her parent's wishes,
inwardly, she has distanced herself.) The more the child pulls away,
the more the parent resorts to the old tactics, only producing more
strain in the relationship. The push-pull cycle continues, as each
generation oils the process.

The result of this self-perpetuating cycle is that parents do not
get what they most crave—power. To the contrary, they experience
more intense feelings of abandonment and greater loss of control
as they are swept away in doubt and anxiety over their children's
devotion and commitment. The problem is that the power and control they want is not really the power and control they think it is.
What they really want from their children is that uniquely gratifying feeling that they are cared about—that they matter. What they
want is love, and love will not blossom in an atmosphere of bossiness. When my father reassures me that it is okay to leave him for a
week's vacation, he reinforces the importance of pleasure in my
life and makes it that much easier for me to be there for him when
he needs me. If he were to assume an authoritarian role and
demand that I have no right to leave him, whether I remain or go,
our relationship has suffered and with it the spirit in which I give
care. The "power" my father has over me is born out of his respect
for my life and needs. Because of his actions, love, not power, is
the foundation of our relationship.

Again and again, I am compelled to return to caregiving as a log-
ical framework for examining the parent-child relationship during
the later years. Because the pain of parents with unmet expectations is heartwrenching and the hurt of perceived abandonment
may be beyond healing, it is necessary to find ways for parents and
children to interact in this stage of life.

By understanding the natural role shifts in the parent-child relationship as it evolves over time, parents who are willing—and I
believe most are—can see to it that their last years are not only joyous but crowned by friendship with their grown children.

Parents *do* hold the keys to paradise, so to speak. Unless they are grown up themselves, they can thwart their children's attempts at being caring and dependable grown children. Dr. Harry J. Berman, writing in the January, 1987 *Journal of Gerontological Social Work* on some of the problems in the grown-child and elderly parent relationship, sums up the crucial role of the parent this way: ". . . parents have a reciprocal obligation, and in an odd way have power over an aspect of their child's development even as they become dependent on the child's help. This power is the power to control the course of the development of filial maturity in their children. Without the help of parents, without the reciprocal development of parental maturity, adult children are powerless to accomplish this important task."[5]

Although in the final words of the preceding chapter I emphasized that children must move forward even if parents will not, the hope is that parents, too, will be active in the tasks that bring parental maturity. The goal, a new parent-child relationship, where parties relate to each other as adults, requires the participation of both generations. It is worth the hard work because of its ultimate reward.

Parents must make the big leap from thinking of parenthood as perennial control over their children to looking at it as a pact between equals. What I ask of parents requires flexibility and courage. But parents are up to the task because, to quote family therapist Dr. Lee Headley, ". . . the key factor is the need of the older parent to maintain a vital link to his adult child, or adult children, for a number of reasons: to maintain a sense of belonging, to have a sense of participating in ongoing life through their grandchildren, to guard against loneliness, to feel that the difficult and unchartered task of parenting was successful, to have a sense of warmth and exchange with their adult child."[6]

The story of Sarah and her children which started in Chapter 2. illustrates how one parent gathered the courage and strength to change the relationship with her daughter. Sarah, who was initially rigid in refusing reconciliation with her daughter, Lois, eventually decided to give it a try. Sarah realized that someone had to make the first move and opted to be the one, giving up the power for the joys of love. She began a process that not only reclaimed her relationship with Lois but elevated it to a level of maturity and gratification not possible when each was younger.

When Sarah first came for counseling, her complaints focused on depression and loneliness. In no time at all, she began telling me about her life, her shattered dreams, and her children.

Raised by an emotionally witholding and verbally abusive mother, Sarah was determined to do things differently with her daughter. But she was doomed, as all parents are, to make mistakes (see the introductory quote to Chapter 3). Sarah made different mistakes from her mother. Because Sarah tried to give Lois all the love and nurturing she never received from her mother and to shelter Lois from the particular brand of pain to which she was subjected, Lois reached adulthood with a self-centered and dependent orientation to life. Sarah did not mean for Lois to turn out this way. It happened only because Sarah wanted Lois to have it better than she did—a goal not at all out of the ordinary for parents to have for their children. As a result, Lois grew up, to use Sarah's words, "indulgent, ungrateful, and selfish." Now on her third husband and fifth job, and with three late-adolescent children, Lois, as is her custom, manages to wade through life with her head barely above water. "I don't know how she does it," Sarah said,

> She's not at all like me—strong-willed and self-reliant. Throughout all her marital fiascos, she never hesitated to ask me for a loan or if I would take the kids for a few weeks in the summer. I spoiled her good and rotten. Now, finally, that things are working out for her with *this* husband and not working out so well for me, in that I'm lonely, depressed, and in so much pain from my arthritis, I really need her and would like her to call and visit. I haven't seen her in over a year. Do you think she really cares about her widowed and alone mother? No way, she only cares about herself! And I made her what she is! Sure, my intentions were good. I wanted to spare her the hurt I got from my mother as I was growing up. Instead, I created a monster. I must say, though, she is a happy monster—always cheerful, without a care in the world. And why should she have any cares! She always got what she wanted—from me, and when one husband didn't work out, she always found another. She's charming, alright! I'll say that for her; with a smile that would melt you. You'd just love her, really, and tell me I'm crazy to find so many faults.

And so it would go with Sarah in session after session, as she would regale me with stories about Lois and her son, Chuck.

Because he was her son, and as Sarah put it, "sons disappear into their wives' families," Chuck did not elicit the same concerns as Lois. Her major complaint about Chuck, a successful businessman in Philadelphia, was that he was not terribly generous with his money; that it would not hurt him a "squeak" if he now and then parted with a few dollars to help pay her dental bills. What is different about Sarah's relationship with Chuck is that Sarah did, indeed, ask him for assistance with her dental bill, and Chuck graciously mailed a check. Sarah could not be open the same way with Lois, however. In Sarah's eyes, asking Lois for help was equivalent to weakness. Because of their intense emotional involvement, colored primarily by anger, hurt, and power plays, Sarah was unable to be as freely expressive to her daughter. There was no way she wanted Lois to know how much she really wanted her affection and friendship. There was no way she could let herself tell Lois of her anguish over having failed to finish better with her than she did with her own mother; or disclose her deep fear that she was becoming a clone of her mother.

Sarah's mind was filled with myths about her children. True, Chuck would only give when asked, but he gave. True, Lois was self-centered and spoiled, but was she really without empathy for Sarah? What was behind Sarah's dark impressions of her daughter and son? The main threads running through Sarah's life history provide clues.

Sarah grew up in a family where she was not only psychologically abused but, as the first-born daughter of four children, saddled with adult responsibilities at an early age. She grew into womanhood with a stunted capacity to trust. Reinforcing her basic distrust and fear of others, at age 20 Sarah married Lou, a man as cold and emotionally witholding as her mother. Lou went a step further by witholding money from Sarah, forcing her to beg or manipulate to obtain what was needed for her family. As a result, when Lois and Chuck were finally in school all day, Sarah went to work. Starting as a secretary in a small lumber company that grew rapidly in the post-World-War-II economy, Sarah rose to general office manager in only a year. She made enough money to give Lois and Chuck music lessons and help finance their way through college.

Although Sarah's work gave her pleasure and fulfillment, her marriage did not. Her husband continued to be tightfisted, besides having numerous extramarital affairs that he shamelessly flaunted. She and Lou fought constantly and, although Sarah wanted a divorce, she said she "was raised to believe that divorce is a sin and besides, those days were different from now."

When Lou suddenly died after a massive coronary, Sarah was understandably not that forlorn. As a fairly young widow of 52 without someone who made her feel inadequate and undeserving, for the first time in her life, Sarah felt free to be herself. She traveled, went to the theater and concerts, dined and played cards with friends, became active in community and church affairs, and enjoyed an almost ten-year relationship with a younger man, whose untimely death left her devastated.

Interspersed between Sarah's joys and adventures, however, were Lois' marital problems and her generally chaotic life. Sarah, true to her established pattern of rescuing Lois, was always available to her to lend an ear, advance a loan, or take the kids off her hands when she was feeling overwhelmed. Totally fused with Lois' life and problems, Sarah's own needs were secondary to Lois's. Whatever Sarah's personal plans or agenda—from attending a meeting to spending a weekend with a friend or going to the theater—they could be dropped at a moment's notice for Lois.

"I've been a good mother to her all her life and never gotten anything back. Now when I need her she isn't there for me. No way will I call her! She knows I'm old and lonely. She can call me to find out how I am! She owes me that." And so it would go on and on, with mounting resentment and anger. "Besides," Sarah would say over and over again, as though to convince herself of its truth, "I manage very well without her!"

Those who know Sarah can say, Yes, she manages well. External appearances indicate Sarah has friends, plays cards, attends religious services, sees movies and plays, and takes classes in line dancing. These activities clearly show Sarah's capacity to reach out to life—to create her own meaningful reality—but I hasten to add that they are not enough.

Sarah needs her daughter's affirmation of love and committment. More than this, however, as Lee Headley tells us, Sarah needs to know that she has somehow done a good job of being a parent. Erik and Joan Erikson, in their book, *Vital Involvement in Old Age*, directly address the meaning of parenting in the life of the elderly person. Considering it part of the process in which the parent measures the value of his or her life in terms of achievement and what will be left behind (immortality), the Eriksons say the following, based on interviews with a sampling of older people in the San Francisco area: "For most of these people, it seems that parenthood has been the primary focus of adulthood responsibility. It is not surprising, therefore, that it is through reconsidering their children's adulthood successes and failures that they seek, retroactively, to validate the responsible caring they themselves provided in their years of active parenting."[7]

Sarah needs her daughter's version of their mutual history to illuminate and interpret the meaning of her strong but tumultuous relationship with Lois. What about Lois can Sarah take pride in? What lessons, if any, taught to Lois by Sarah did she incorporate into her life? What will Lois remember about Sarah when Sarah is dead? What does their relationship mean to Lois? And finally, did Sarah somehow succeed in being a better mother than her own mother?

Only through contact with Lois will Sarah be able to find the answers to these questions, penetrating the core meaning of her relationship with her daughter and the meaning of her own life. To find peace with herself, Sarah must have clear answers. An open dialogue, emotionally honest, it cannot be governed by inappropriate and irrelevant rules.

Sarah and Lois will always be mother and daughter, but they must reunite as friends. As Dr. Emily Hancock writes in her book, *The Girl Within*, they must together "transform a critical tie," changing an earlier unequal relationship into another, where mother and daughter as peers relate to each other with mutual respect.[8] In other words, Sarah and Lois must elevate their relationship to a higher, more mature level. In this instance, both were grown up enough to meet the challenge.

What was apparent to me through the years Sarah and I worked together was an implicit softness in Sarah's outwardly unyielding attitude toward Lois. Critical though she was, Sarah managed to pepper her harsh comments with kind words about Lois's charm, her sense of humor, her cheerful disposition, and her ability to survive. This soft core told me there was hope for cordial relations.

I pointed out to Sarah how her positive statements about Lois contradicted her overall condemnation of her. Sarah at first denied it. After a time, denial became pleasant surprise as Sarah realized that Lois was like her in more than a few respects. During one of our sessions, Sarah was bragging about how Lois, through perseverance, landed a hard-to-get position with an advertising company. "You know, she's got my spunk after all, Sarah said." "Spunk" turned to "guts" as it dawned on Sarah that, were she married to Lou now, she would certainly divorce him. And at one point, she considered that she, like Lois, might also be on her third husband.

Once she began thinking of Lois as someone like her, with strength, spunk, and guts, and once she was able to understand that these traits manifest themselves differently in Lois, Sarah began to see her in a different light. At this crucial point, it also occurred to Sarah that if Lois did not value her, she would never have fostered the warm and loving relationship between Sarah and her grandchildren. Said Sarah, rather incredulously, "Her kids and I have the best relationship. I know that when I die they will miss me and talk about me to their kids. They write and call me, even if she doesn't. Just talking about my attachment to my grandchildren makes me feel better than I've felt in years."

While listening to Sarah rave about her grandchildren and their devotion to her, I could only think that perhaps pay back—the "you owe me"—for Sarah was meant to come through the medium of her grandchildren. That if Lois, for whatever reason, could not express love and thanks, then at least Lois's children could. Though a generation removed, perhaps this delayed response would satisfy Sarah. But I was dead wrong. Sarah was *not* satisfied. She wanted and, indeed, saw to it that she got more. In an act of pure courage, she telephoned Lois.

With unabashed candor, she told Lois she was too old to play games, that she would like to see her, and that she hoped they might be friends in whatever time was left to her. She told Lois she was flying out to see her right away.

Sarah and Lois met, talked, and conquered the myths that had emotionally separated them for so many years. Myths or half-truths, unless confronted, have the power to last a lifetime and to taint memories after a parent dies.

Sarah and Lois got it straight while each was in the arena of the living. Face to face, they brushed away all the cobwebs of confusion, misunderstanding, and guesswork that had blurred their perception of each other as whole human beings.[9]

As a result of Sarah's daring, she had to give up beliefs she held as inviolable—beliefs about Lois not loving her; that she herself was blameless in perpetuating the estrangement with her daughter; beliefs about Lois' basic ungratefulness and selfishness. For both Sarh and Lois the process of accepting each as she is was painful.

Sarah winced when Lois revealed that she was always aware that Sarah saw her as a failure. She smarted even more when Lois expressed rage at Sarah for her inability to accept her as she was and to give her encouragement and support, other than financial, during her hard times. Unable all these years to tell Sarah her feelings because of fear of further disapproval and rejection, Lois became even angrier. Withholding thanks and appreciation as a way to seek revenge upon Sarah, she overtly behaved as ingrate while inwardly feeling ashamed over her dependency. Despite Lois's resentment, however, she ultimately told Sarah that she still loved and admired her, and that all her life she wanted nothing more than to be like her.

With souls bared, each revealed secrets, disclosed feelings of shame, and chased away ghosts that had hovered between them for so long. By the time Sarah returned home, a terrible weight had been lifted from her back. She felt that she now understood her daughter as a whole person and knew Lois understood her in the same way. The issues that divided them dimmed in importance. Eclipsed by the love and respect that "transformed the critical tie," their disagreements, conflicts, and disappointments became a means to forge genuine understanding of each other, to unearth all that bound them together as different adults who happen to be mother and daughter.

Two instructive themes emerge from the the Sarah-Lois story. The first, echoing premises developed in Chapter 2, relates to the interdependence of generations. The second is another dimension of interdependence that strongly affects the kind and amount of care elderly parents expect from their middle-aged children.

Within the context of what it means to be adult, the story of Sarah and Lois underscores the permanence of the ties between the generations. No matter what wounds and misdeeds scar our family histories or the tears and heartache they bring, parents and children are bound together. To deny that we are connected with our parents or our children is to deny that we are whole human beings.

Sarah and Lois needed each other's acceptance and expression of love. Although Lois could have managed without Sarah's blessings, when they came to her life was considerably richer. Reconnected with Sarah after many years of estrangement, Lois got back an important part of her identity that let her feel like a whole person. Once she accepted how she was like her mother and how she was unique, Lois had grown up.

Referring to mothers and daughters, Dr. Hancock further writes in *The Girl Within*, "They (daughters) were reaching not for simple independence but for interdependence—a kind of rapproachment that marks relationships of equal give-and-take." Echoing what we said in Chapter 2, Dr. Hancock adds, "Their (her respondents') accounts call into question the normalcy and utility of a psychological standard that rests on separation, suggesting that a model that requires adults to separate from their parents is itself an odd one. In fact, separation would seem to be a crude 'solution' to a 'problem' the culture itself has fabricated."[10] Dr. Hancock believes that all grown children, regardless of gender, wish to "change the tie without eliminating it; to refashion the relationship so that it fit who they'd become." Sarah and Lois not only changed the tie but strengthened it to a degree not possible when Lois was "little" and Sarah "big" and "powerful."

For Sarah, interdependence provided the gratifying reward of seeing her own character and personality traits passed on to the next generation. Lois was feisty, courageous, and unabashedly honest, just like Sarah. Sarah took great pride in these characteristics and in the knowledge that they would be carried on through the generations. They also freed Sarah from worry, because she now felt reassured that Lois, like her mother, would always be able to take care of herself.

For other parents, it may be a child's artistic or mechanical ability, sense of humor, energy, or pleasant disposition that has meaning in terms of their ongoing life. Although these characteristics may have been noticed when children were younger, they become more important as elderly parents reflect upon how they will be remembered and what about themselves will be passed on to the next generation.

My dear friend, Marjorie, is a superb cook, as was her mother before her and her daughter now. For Marjorie, her 3-year-old granddaughter Julia's love of food represents a meaningful carryover. "Look at her, will you!" exclaims Marjorie. "She eats with the same gusto as I do. And she knows the name of every dish she likes to eat at the Chinese restaurant. And one day, she'll have my appreciation of fine food too. And she'll tell her children where that came from, from me, her grandmother!" Here again, immortality surfaces in its many guises. Immortality does not just belong to the rich, who insure it with bequests to universities or museums that place their names on plaques. It is accessible to everyone who understands the importance of interdependence in life. As the Eriksons tell us, "Before we were, there were ancestors. When we leave, there will be descendants and or memorable deeds and accomplishments."[11]

The second theme that the Sarah-Lois story plays out is more specific than the concept of the interdependence of the generations. It relates directly to the caregiving relationship between parent and child, and it is critically important because it can hurt the quality of the whole relationship. This second form of interdependence requires that parents facing the dependencies of old age trust others, both relatives and outsiders, paid or unpaid, as caretakers. The Eriksons remind us that as the infant must develop trust to survive, so must the elderly. "When physical fraility demands assistance, one must accept again an appropriate dependence without the loss of trust and hope. The old, of course, are not endowed with the endearing survival skills of the infant. Old bodies are more difficult to care for, and the task itself is less satisfying to the caretaker than that of caring for infants. . . . Only a lifetime of slowly developing trust is adequate to meet this situation, which so naturally elicits despair and disgust and at one's helplessness. Of how many elders could one say, 'He surrendered every vestige of his old life with a sort of courteous, half humorous gentleness?'"[12]

Sarah's and Lois's encounter was infinitely meaningful for them. Sarah, who had spent her entire life concerned about people's motives and believing the worst of human nature, finally allowed herself to trust. In so doing, she finally crossed the Rubicon into adulthood at age 75. No one achieves adulthood without mastering trust. Trusting in the kindness and good will of others allows graceful, courageous aging.

What this tells us is that the degree to which the elderly person can be interdependent with others is related to his or her capacity to trust. When Sarah opened herself to her daughter, she established an interdependency with her that transformed their relationship. Defined by give and take and mutual respect, the new relationship could encompass Sarah's vulnerability without threatening her sense of self. She could now come to Lois in need; she could ask Lois for appropriate support without feeling in a one-down position. She trusted that Lois would be there for her with genuine understanding and without sitting in judgment. Interdependency with Lois enriched Sarah's world. She felt the warmth of connection with her daughter and a sense of belonging to Lois's family. She felt that after all her misgivings about the kind of parent she was, she had raised a good daughter and was a better mother than her mother.

Interdependency with a grown child, however, does not necessarily signal the achievement of complete interdependency. What we need is a more complete version of this concept. The caregiving relationship between parent and child once again becomes a useful model.

To be truly interdependent, a parent must be able to respond positively to help from strangers when this kind of support is necessary. Such interdependence, however, is not easy to achieve in a society where independence, is generally regarded as a supreme virtue.[13] As a result, some parents, feeling shame over their neediness, either reject all assistance outright or look for help from family members rather than expose themselves to outsiders. I say to these misguided parents, "You have a right to your dependencies. They do not signal failure or shame. Get the help you need and deserve, only please don't count too much on your children."

With grown children busier than ever, parents who count on them to be on permanent call usually are disappointed and can feel abandoned. The end result can be disastrous, whatever the reason for refusing outside support—a cultural attitude preaching independence, a family norm dictating no strangers for parent care, or a parent's deep-seated belief that children "owe" them care. Although the parent may badger and use guilt to force a child into giving care, the care will lack the joy and love necessary to healthy caregiving. Tinged with anger and resentment, this kind of care creates emotional strain between parent and child.

On the other hand, elderly parents who have the capacity to be interdependent enjoy closer and more satisfying relationships with their children. Leaving as many services and supports as possible in the hands of outsiders, they depend on their children for the "being with" instead of the "doing for." Releasing their children from the time-consuming and physically exhausting chores of cooking, shopping, marketing, transportation, and bathing, they give them the extra energy for the important aspect of caregiving—emotional involvement. Take for example, the rewards that come to the mother who prefers to use senior transportation for weekly marketing, freeing her daughter for a long visit with her later that day or week. Compare them with the aftermath that follows another mother's insistence that her daughter help her with this chore.

The interdependent mother has the opportunity to exercise autonomy over her life by depending on herself to find and choose a service that fills her need. She also creates a space where she and her daughter can spend meaningful time. Instead of sitting in a car while driving to the market, walking up and down the aisles to select food, carrying packages into the kitchen, unloading bags of groceries, and filling the refrigerator, this mother and daughter can spend a few hours together talking about things that matter to them. Certainly, there is a closeness born of doing everyday chores together. In strained parent-child relationships it may be the only means to create closeness. It can, however, become a goal in itself, shutting out more intimate ways of being together.

Parents can use time differently when they do not have to depend on their children for this kind of support. They and their children can control time in a sense. They can fill it with shared concerns, reminiscences, or funny stories that have the potential to become sustaining memories for as long as they live. Indeed, fragments of a memorable encounter may become precious legacies passed on through the generations.

Jerry, whose parents are lucky enough to have sufficient financial resources to live in a retirement community, speaks of how wonderful visiting with them is because "all we have to do is just enjoy one another, to sit and talk about ourselves, the grandchildren, politics, old friends, and the great times we had and are having right now just being together. But it's definitely the stories my family is hearing from my folks when we're together that we'll never forget and that will be passed on."

Paradoxically, then, the more the elderly person can rely on the kindness of strangers for necessary assistance, the more he or she will be able to exert control over his or her environment. This is best illustrated by my friend's 75-year-old wheelchair-bound father, who sits in his home day after day because he refuses to allow his paid companion, a genial, caring man of infinite patience, to take him places. Ashamed of his dependence and not trusting this outsider with his car or his welfare, he has neither the freedom nor independence of someone with a similar problem who can accept his need for help. Unlike Miss Daisy of the film, *Driving Miss Daisy*, he misses out on the possibility of making a devoted friend, an insider, out of his companion.

An 82-year-old woman I know is a perfect example of the reverse attitude. Severely disabled with Parkinson's disease, she still loves inviting friends to lunch or dinner and having parties. Because she is not embarrassed to ask her guests to bring a dish or to lend a hand in the kitchen, she can entertain company in her home. Relinquishing control to others—interdependence—lets her continue to enrich her life while still being mistress of her fate.

The concept of relinquishment runs through old age like the yellow brick road. As we get older, we are constantly in the process of giving up. We give up whatever depends on "physical aptitudes or was concerned with biological needs."[14] Simply stated, we give up running for walking, fast walking for slow walking, hikes for short treks. And so it goes, until one day we may have to give up walking itself. Or we give up eating spicy foods for plainer fare, heaping plates for mere tastes of this or that. The relinquishment process continues as we journey through life.

As people pass through the stages of loss that mark growing old, Else Frenkel-Brunswik tells us they must have the ability to "transpose" themselves, to take on other attitudes toward life that meet their new needs and losses.[15] The elderly person must, in essence, "transpose" his or her identity so that it depends less on biological nature and more on activities and interests directed by ideals and practical concerns. Even in more-primitive societies, the ability to transpose is recognized as a basic requirement for healthy aging.[16] Dr. David Guttman, professor of psychology at the University of Michigan, found in his research on the Highland Maya of Mexico that the elders in this culture, like our own, define their identities in terms of passive pursuits such as the cultivation and enjoyment of family and friends instead of the active pursuits of production, competition, achievement, and work.

Yet, one of the hardest transpositions for the elderly is the adaptation of a dramatically different parental role. The earlier role, the one that parents were accustomed to for so long, no longer works when children are adults. Defined by nurturing and protection and authoritarian in nature, it has outlived its usefulness. Parents must opt for a new role that will enhance and enrich relationships with their children.

In Asian cultures, primarily Oriental and Indian, where elders by tradition are valued for their gifts of wisdom and spirituality, the shift to a new kind of parent is effortless. The earlier role of nurturer and protector easily yields to the more exalted role of teacher or sage as a natural rite of passage. Children and grandchildren look to the venerable "old head" for guidance and spiritual counsel. Esteemed for the special gifts only a long life can bestow, the elderly parent occupies a place of honor in the family unit. These cultures may hold significant clues to the nature of the new parental role that is required. Parents could turn to these traditions to discover more meaningful ways to be parents when their children are adults.

A popular idea today focuses on old age as a "third age" of man.[17] Beginning at age 60 and considered a fertile period when the elderly can return to society their unique wisdom and knowledge, the "third age" gives elders further opportunities for contribution and growth. In the earlier two ages (age one beginning with birth and ending at age 25; age two starting at 25 and ending at 60) emphasis is on building, pursuing, competing, and achieving. The third age has the potential for something more subtle in nature—it can become a viable model for transposition to a more appropriate parental role. Applied in this narrower sense, a parent could use what he or she has learned throughout life to provide his or her grown children with guidance and fresh perspectives on many of their daily struggles. Like the elder of Asian cultures, the parent becomes a teacher or mentor.

The wisdom of "third-age" parents, offered at critical times, may bring balance to the lives of ambitious offspring who, in pursuing material success have forgotten their values. Weeding out the vanities from what really matters, parents could be of enormous help to children on the fast track. Loving friends and family, extending kindness to others, and appreciating the here and now are the basics of living of which young people sometimes need to be reminded. The late philosopher and professor Abraham J. Heschel says it best when he warns us, "We have nearly lost the art of conveying to our children our power to praise, our ability to cherish the things that cannot be quantified."[18]

Though life today is more complex and pressured than it was in the past, the disappointments, sadness, and frustrations that accompany making it from one day to the next are timeless. When tragedy strikes the world of a grown child, parents frequently can give great comfort. One woman said the following of her 78-year-old mother after her teenaged daughter was killed in an auto accident:

> My mother gave my husband and me the courage to go on with our lives. She made us understand with all the right words that the loss of our daughter, though something that would leave its scar, did not mean our lives were over. She was somehow always there for us, no matter how angry or bitter we were. And believe me, there were times when she became the target for all our misery and despair. She always seemed to understand, though. She never told us to stop our grieving, our crying. She never said that enough is enough. Whatever we felt was okay. Because Mom herself had survived so many losses—my father and her only sister—we knew she understood exactly what we were going through. She gave us something our friends could not—unconditional understanding and love. Our friends, though loving and well-meaning, had not lived and experienced all that she had. Most important, though, she was a living example of hope and courage.

It is not only necessary but natural to give up the role of parent that made sense when children were young. Without diminishing the importance of the earlier role, parents have yet another chance to profoundly affect their chidren's lives. Because their children are now mature enough to want to hear what they have to say, to have respectful conversations, to value guidance that is offered, and to appreciate the wisdom parents can bring to their lives, the third-age role brings rich rewards.

How wonderful it is for the parent whose grown child comes as an equal looking for counsel or to share an insight or experience. How satisfying it is for a parent to be needed this way. This kind of encounter is far better than a parent saying I know more than you, and intruding into a child's life.

One of the benefits of this new role comes when parents realize that although they have much to teach their children, they also can learn from them. In his book, *The Road Less Traveled*, Dr. Scott Peck notes that, "Parents who are unwilling to risk the suffering of changing and growing and learning from their children are choosing a path of senility—whether they know it or not—and their children and the world will leave them far behind. Learning from their children is the best opportunity most people have to assure themselves of a meaningful old age. Sadly, most do not take this opportunity.[19]

Believing that as parents we know it all, closes the door to some of the most exciting encounters we can have with our grown children. Betty, a 91-year-old great-grandmother who lives in an assisted-living community, describes her relationship with her family in these words:

> I cannot wait for my children and grandchildren to visit. I love to hear all their stories about what they are doing, seeing, and feeling about this idea or that. When they come, my sitting room here is filled with constant chatter. One of my grandaughters lives with her boyfriend, and though at first I didn't like the idea, I now believe it makes sense. He visits me too! Things have really changed for women, you know. Had I been born later, I would have done things differently. Not that I regret a minute of my life, but I would have lived a fuller one. I have four granddaughters, and they all work. One is an engineer who travels all over the world. Another is an environmentalist in Washington, D.C., and two are nurses in big hospitals. I have great-grandchildren who are teenagers. You should see the way they wear their hair and dress! When they visit I feel so alive. We talk about everything, from politics to sex. I can't read or see television any more as much as I like, and it's my children who

keep me up to date. We disagree about lots, but I feel that as long as my mind is open to them I am never really old.

Betty loves to hear about what is current and keeps up-to-date through those meetings with her family. She does not feel painfully isolated or left out. And, most important, she is right when she says, "I am never really old." When parents are open to learning from their children, a powerful regenerative force keeps them young in the only places where it counts—heart, mind, and spirit.

Maturity, in its fullest meaning, is about movement and transition; about reaching out to new ideas, concepts, and relationships; about flexibility instead of rigidity. Successful aging and openess to growth, essentially, are one and the same.

Current research supports the idea that older people have the potential to learn, grow, create, and deepen relationships as long as they live. The research of Gay Gaer Luce, for example, which led to the development of SAGE (Senior Actualization and Growth Explorations) programs throughout America, clearly shows that old age marks the beginning of a new richness in living.[20] Emphasizing that old age is a fundamental part of the human life cycle, in her book, *Your Second Life*, Dr. Luce challenges us to be all that we can possibly be in our later years. Her call to live as fully as possible in whatever time is left is both exciting and hopeful.

The richness of old age is derived in great part from satisfying relationships with children. As the Eriksons point out, many parents evaluate their lives through the fortunes and misfortunes of their children. Not all parents receive gratification from their children because they may be displeased with their lifestyles, choice of mate, or beliefs. It is possible, however, for parents to transcend these external ego identities for more universal ones.

Bill's case is an apt illustration. Although for years Bill was angry and bitterly disappointed over the homosexuality of his 50-year-old lawyer-son, Ed, in late life he was able to put this aside and see more than the way Ed chose to live. Seeing Ed for the decent, caring, and courageous person he was, Bill finally welcomed Ed and his mate into his home and eventually traveled with them to Scotland to visit family members he wanted to see before he died. No longer judgmental of the externals of Ed's life-style, Bill found a closeness and pleasure in their relationship he did not believe possible.

Let me say emphatically, as I do to all parents who are finished with the consuming and arduous years of child rearing, "Get a life beyond the lives of your children! Your children's lives are not yours, anyway." With life expectancy at an all-time high and early retirement a reality for many, life holds more exciting possibilites than ever before. It is not too late to pursue those interests and hobbies you sacrificed years ago or even to consider new careers. Besides that, the more parents are involved in their own lives, the less they will invade their children's worlds and the more they will enjoy relationships with them. Depending upon themselves for entertainment, recreation, or stimulation, they require less of their overburdened and busy children.

When identity is no longer defined solely by parenthood but by other meaningful interests, activities, and inner resources, control or domination of children for a sense of self-worth and usefulness becomes unnecessary. Dr. Paul Arthur Schilpp, distinguished research professor of philosophy emeritus at Southern Illinois University, sums it up best of all. Quoting from Phillip Berman's anthology, *The Courage to Grow Old*, Dr. Schilpp notes:

> If you are in misery at the task you perform eight hours a day—whether that's watching tv in retirement or punching a clock at a factory—life isn't worthwhile. Get out and do something else. And it's no secret that unhappy souls usually exit sooner than happy ones. . . . just as important we need to enjoy and care for other people. . . . such caring does not mean that we should expect too much from our children and grandchildren. Don't expect them to attend to you out of gratitude. Rather, let love come to you free of guilt and lead your own life. Make your own new friends and go about your business.[21]

He was 92 when he wrote these words.

Society cries for the talents of wise old heads. Whether to teach, to serve, or to care, third-age parents are in the singular position of being able to enrich the lives of others. Never was time more ripe for what has come to be called "creative retirement." With people today not only retiring earlier, but better-educated and healthier, there is no limit to how those over 65 can spend the rest of their lives.[22] Although some wish to play, others wish to engage in activities that "inspire purpose to life," to quote Dr. Harry Moody, deputy director of the Brookdale Center on Aging.[23] Whether on the golf course or at the University of North Carolina Center for Creative Retirement in Asheville, North Carolina, where retirees can pursue active community-centered studies and services, there is ample opportunity for everyone to do his or her own thing.

"We're looking at new roles older people are playing and new norms of what it means to be an older person," said Dr. Ronald J. Manheimer, director of the University of North Carolina's center.[24] People living to age 65, no longer hemmed in by obsolete stereotypes, have more control over how they wish to shape their lives than ever before. In a real sense they can have it all. They can be appropriately involved parents and grandparents, while at the same time integrating these family concerns with those of a broader, more humanitarian nature. 'Tis a far cry, indeed, from the sixteenth century, when Shakespeare described the seventh stage of man as " ... second childishness and mere oblivion, sans teeth, sans eyes, sans taste, sans every thing."[25]

Parents who are fully grown up, therefore, have friends and interests that reach beyond the family. As third-age parents, they share with their children the adventures, joys, and challenges of their new lives, while relating to them as peers. Third-age parents did for and gave to their children as best they could, found both happiness and pain in the process of raising them, and now expect their children to live their own lives.

Anne, 70, who moved to Arizona after her husband died 12 years ago, epitomizes the attitude and sensibilities of a third-age parent. Addressing the issue of what her children owe her, she related the following:

> Of my four chidren, only my son lives nearby in Phoenix. He calls me every week, but he and his family are busy, and I see them whenever they have the time. My other three children all live a distance away. My older daughter lives in Hawaii and my younger one never left our hometown in Indiana. My other son lives in New York City, but since he travels coast to coast so much on business, I am able to see him for little visits five to six times a year. But I know my children care; I know they will be there for me if necessary. Whenever we're together we have a marvelous time. Distance does not detract from our closeness. My mother spent the last four years of her life in a nursing home, and for all I know I may have to do

the same. I've thought about my future a lot, and know I never want to live with any of my children. In the meantime as long as I have my health, friends, and this wonderful part-time job (Anne is a sales person in a fashionable boutique), I live a full and happy life. What do my children owe me? I suppose I can say nothing, really. Wait! Respect, certainly. And of course, I want to know they care, which they do. But they must live their own lives. That's what it's all about.

Although the transition to third-age parent seemed effortless for Anne, for others the passage may be more difficult. Change is seldom easy and often quite scary. It is especially hard to relinquish a parental role that has been comfortable for so long. Yet, to everything there is a season. And although old age is often called the season of loss, much is missed by referring to it only in these terms. For there are also sweet gains. Among them are a new and more gratifying way to be a parent in this vintage season of life and the inner peace that accompanies acceptance of children for doing and being the best they could.

The capacity for the parent to change is there, as is the motivation. All it takes is courage. And that, of course, only grows with age.

Dancing Solo

During the last 10 years of my mother's life, I imagined the two of us together in a dance where she gently led me through passages that were unfamiliar and scary. Although she was the leader in this dance, knowing all the time which direction to pursue, we moved together as partners. She never used her vast knowledge of what lay ahead for me to intimidate me. And when she became tired, because after all, she was old and frail, she graciously allowed me to lead her. As long as we moved together, helping each other, everything would be alright. I was at peace.

The image of us dancing was so powerful that I wrote about it in my journal and even dreamed about it. Of course, the image's significance was clear. My mother was my teacher. She was teaching me what all elderly parents must, if they can, teach their children—how to grow old and die with grace and courage. And I was truly blessed to have such a good teacher. Whatever she did not give me when I was younger—only because she *could* not—she more than made up for with this final gift.

When I was trying to figure out what to call children who are not as lucky as I, children who will neither know the unique pleasures of friendship with aging parents nor have parents from whom to learn life's final lessons, I decided to call them "solo dancers." Unlike children who deliberately cut off from their mothers and fathers, solo dancers crave connection. They *want* to help their parents appropriately; they *want* to be the recipients of their wisdom, and they *want* warm exchange. The problem is that some parents are not able to do their share. Because they refuse to yield the power of the parental role, insisting that all transactions take place on their terms, children are denied the closeness they wish. And because power does not create an atmosphere where parents and children can share heartfelt concerns, children are left in the dark about what it feels like to grow old and face death.

Dave's comments about his 78-year-old father capture the Catch-22 nature of the dilemma:

> When I tell Dad, who sits home alone day after day, that I cannot take him to the bank, barber, and lunch on Tuesday but would be delighted to do it Wednesday, he tells me he's busy then and I should forget it. Then when I rearrange my schedule to accommodate him, there's never a word of thanks or recognition for what I've done. I'm always angry with him because he has to have it his way. I would like to spend more time with him, to feel closer, because he can be a sweet guy, but how can I when he always has to pull these power trips. We waste so damn much time arguing about garbage when we could really enjoy each other.

Solo dancers have positive feelings about their parents. Like Dave, they care. Were they, like flagrantly physically or psychologically abused children, able to detest their parents without ambivalence, their lot would be easier. They could then cooly withdraw from the scene, without guilt or a regretful glance backward. Things are far more difficult for solo dancers, who, as they recall their childhoods and early adult years are able to summon up warm memories of family life and positive characteristics in parents. Genuinely wanting to give care from good will rather than moral obligation, they are frustrated and anguished by their parents' stiff-necked attitude.

Although most of these children carry on the rest of their lives quite competently, all of them feel something remains unfinished. In counseling I see a deep sadness over the loss of anticipated intimacy with parents at this turning point in both their lives. Wanting and able to be there for them with respect and love, they are met with ungratefulness. Trying again and again to talk it out with parents, they are met with inflexibility. Wanting friendship, warmth, and an honest exchange of feelings, they are met with intimidation. Their parents, unable to find meaning in the hard but natural losses of old age or to let go of old resentments, essentially lacking in wisdom, not only push them further away but serve as poor role models.

My friend Joan, 49, is the prototype of these children. As senior vice-president of a large personnel counsulting firm, strikingly beautiful and genuinely sweet, she appears to have it all. Yet, unfinished business with her 80-year-old mother, who lives in Florida, remains a deep hurt. She tells it like this:

> I have been trying for five years now to patch things up with my mother. Growing up, I always felt close to her, we did things together, and she was a support to me. She's generally a teriffic lady— worked until just a year ago, was able to begin a new life as a widow, and has lots of friends. But as far as she and I are concerned either there's no way I can ever do enough for her or when I offer help she refuses it. There's no way I can score points with her. If I call her, for example, two times a week, it should be four times; if it's every day, it ought to be twice a day. And when I offered to help hang her drapes in her new apartment the last time I visited, she refused, but in the next breath moaned she had no one to help her. It's all got to be on her terms. My older brother, who lives near her, does not have these problems. I'm the only daughter and she has an entirely different list of expectations for me.
>
> Five years ago when I had a hysterectomy, our rift deepened. My children were in college, I was divorced, and I asked her to come stay with me for a week. I was all alone. Because she was healthy and vigorous, well able to afford the travel expenses, and I really needed her, I knew she could handle the whole thing. Well, she wouldn't come; she didn't understand the necessity of my wanting her. She told me I have lots of friends who can take care of me. No matter how I tried to explain—and believe me it was through plenty of tears—that I needed her just to be there for me, she couldn't get it. She minimized my hurt, never really understanding where I was coming from. I was so angry that for several months we stopped speaking to each other. My brother dismisses the whole thing with, 'Joan, to her a hysterectomy is like having your ears pierced. That's the way she is. You'll have to understand and forgive her.' Of course, were it the other way around and she needed me, I would come running. And she would expect me to come running if she did, in fact, have her ears pierced!
>
> Well, over all these years I have forgiven her and do understand

how she is. I have also been able to tell her of my hurt, even though she couldn't come forth with any acknowledgment. I visit her and when I'm there I try to talk to her about what still troubles me. We get nowhere. She says, 'I can't understand what it is you want from me and what there is to talk about. You know how much I love you and how much I always have.' She denies and denies and yet when I invite her to come to my daughter's engagement party in Dallas next month, she says she won't because *I* don't really want her there. And when I ask her how she can say that, because I do want her there and so does her granddaughter, Alyssa, she just won't talk about it.

I suppose I ask for more than she can give. I'm always disappointed. Sometimes I pick up the phone to call her, dial, and then reconsider. I quickly hang up knowing I'm not going to get what I need, so why bother. It's like I want the chicken soup and she never has it. The metaphor that for me has always described our relationship is like going for brunch in this restaurant, believe it or not, called 'Mothers.' Well, they're supposed to serve until 2 o'clock. If I get there at 1:45, they tell me, 'Sorry, lady, no brunch; but you can have lunch.' Well, I want my mom to give me brunch.

So, there's always this heavy strain between us. We're never light with each other; we never truly enjoy each other.

"What do you think is at bottom of all the strain? Why is it there?" I ask Joan.

After some pause, she answers, "I really feel, deep down, that she doesn't accept me for who I am. If only we could sit down together and talk about our differences and perceptions or misperceptions. If only we could get it all straight. I accept her for who and what she is and I'll take her just that way. I can even accept— can you imagine—her writing a letter to my boyfriend to thank him for taking care of me, because I understand how this gesture makes her feel like a good momma. I don't like it, but it's okay. I can even laugh.

"It's all such a big hurt, such a big hole; and I know that after she dies it will be worse. But I've done all that I could and I suppose she really has, too. I'm sad we won't be able to finish better."

Carol, age 51, relates how it is for her to be the middle-aged child of such "un-wise," power-clinging parents:

They want me for marketing and to go to the butcher, but otherwise want no part of me. They do not want to hear my thoughts, opinions, beliefs on anything. They reject my advice that they sorely need on medical and financial matters. They do not let me into their world as an adult; I am wanted only as a servant. They won't let me know them as people who are getting old and are fearful and worried. The minute I step over the threshold into their home, I feel I am a child again—helpless, dependent, and a know-nothing. How can I ever, Vivian, really grow up into full adulthood without their acknowledgment and their blessings. Soon they will be dead; I would give anything to get it right while they are still alive.

Stuck in a kind of twilight zone, someplace between childhood and adulthood, Carol feels angry, frustrated, and helpless to change her situation.

On a deeply personal level, what children like Joan and Carol experience is an incompleteness of self. Evelyn, a 52-year-old sales representative who cares for her Alzheimer's-stricken mother and frail but controlling father, describes the feeling in these words: "My father's friendship would have somehow rounded out my life. It would be his supreme gift, telling me that I am okay just as I am. It may sound a bit extreme and crazy but his recognition of me as a caring, responsible adult would mean that I have come full circle in my development. I feel that as long as he treats me with that unbending upper hand of his, I will never make the last rung in the ladder to adulthood."

Because it takes two—Evelyn *and* her father, and Joan and Carol and their parents—to engage in this intergenerational dance, its nature is tenuous. Unless *both* generations can relate as adults, that final rounding out, that wholeness they and others like them desire, remains beyond their reach. Consequently, when a child moves in to be appropriately dependable, the parent must not back off. Moving instead to accept, allow, and reward the child's action, parent as partner leads on toward this special final connection.

What about parents, however? Make no mistake, the pain is there for parents as well. As I see it, though, it is generally parents who unwittingly cause their own suffering. Having already lost a major degree of control over their world and fearful of losing yet another hold—dominion over their children—they withold closeness as a way of exercising power.

On the other hand, parents for whom parental control is unnecessary and who have other sources of self-esteem (see Chapter 4) welcome their children to the dance. By asking for assistance in tone and language that convey respect instead of intimidation and, unlike Dave's father, demonstrating sensitivity to their children's needs, they make it a pleasure for children to be dependable. With the exception of children who have been cruelly abused or who, like Roseanne of Chapter 3, remain dependent and immature throughout their lives, I have rarely known a child to reject a parent's sincere request for assistance. As I noted in Chapter 4, in the words of Dr. Berman, parents ". . . have power over an aspect of their child's development even as they become dependent on their child's help. This power is the power to control the course of the development of filial maturity in their children."[1]

Alas, then, even in old age, a parent's work is never done. In addition to the hard tasks of adapting to the losses that are part of growing old, parents still have a final chore. They must give their children the opportunity to be dependable, caring, and responsible adults who would like to make a difference in their parents' limited lives. As children identify with parents in childhood to prepare for the challenges of adulthood, in middle age, children learn from parents how to prepare for the journey to old age and death. The art of graciously letting go, of gentle surrender to others for help and support—to lean upon another body or to grasp another hand—are the valuable lessons our parents must teach us.

Whether this is successful depends on the maturity of parents. Says sociologist Lillian Troll, ". . . the significance of the parent-child relationship does not end with the launching but continues throughout life. The parent who continues to mature throughout life—to accept his own development as meaningful and satisfying—is helping his children to mature in turn."[2]

My friend Barbara, whose mother is paralyzed from her waist down, translates Troll's statement this way: "My mother, always amazing in her resiliency and ability to roll with the punches, is even more amazing at 87! Here she is in a wheelchair, incontinent and dependent upon others for her personal needs, and yet finds meaning and wonder in every day. What guts! I have learned from her that I can, if necessary, be as brave as she." Barbara's mother, wondrously alive in her mind, continues to be a role model for Barbara. She teaches Barbara by her own example that it is possible to grow old with courage and grace. Through her maturity and wisdom, she helps Barbara to mature in turn.

Margaret Blenkner, the gerontologist who originated the concept of "filial maturity" in the 1960s, calls it a bona fide developmental stage—like early childhood, adolescence, middle age, and old age. Occurring at that transition point when parents become dependent upon their children—the filial crisis—it demands that children leave behind the rebelliousness of adolescence and see their parents as people. Turning to a parent again "no longer as a child but as a mature adult with a new role and a different love, they see him for the first time as an individual with his own rights, needs, limitations, and a life history that to a large extent, made him the person he is long before his child existed."[3]

Since Dr. Blenkner also defines filial maturity as dependability, children mature in this sense do not become their parents' parents.[4] What they become instead are dependable adults. Role reversal has no place in Dr. Blenkner's theory. Sons and daughters who believe caring for their parents is the same as taking care of helpless children are not behaving as mature adults in this sense. Children who give care while respecting a parent as a person are. When children turn their parents into infants, parents have every right to pull back from this demeaning treatment. They are being treated as less than equal.

The agonizing paradox for children who dance solo is that most qualify as mature on all Dr. Blenkner's counts. Ready to be dependable and able to see their parents as people, they have almost made it to the last rung of Evelyn's "ladder to adulthood." Although the top is in clear view, they have no parental hand to pull them to the top. They cannot complete their journey.

The following vignette about Molly and her parents illustrates the frustration and pain of the child who, though ready to be mature as a daughter, cannot be because of her parents' unwillingness to participate in the process. Unlike Sarah and Lois in the preceeding chapter who were finally able to work together to achieve mutual understanding and emotional closeness, Molly and her parents cannot find a way to resolve the filial crisis that tears at their family.

Molly and I met when she approached me after I had completed a talk about caregiving children for the civic organization to which she belonged. Excitedly, but with a hint of sadness in her dark eyes, she gently tapped me on the shoulder, saying, "If you want to hear about a family where everything you've talked about comes to life but more so, let me know. And besides, I just have to blurt it out to someone." Finding her openess and warmth irresistible, I took her telephone number and said I would call her to arrange a date.

What Molly told me over lunch on a warm spring day is one of hundreds of stories I have heard about children who tried but failed to reclaim their relationship with a parent or parents.

Molly's story and those that follow are about the efforts of grown children in mid-life to find closeness and understanding and to become mature sons and daughters in their relationships with aging parents. Because women are the assumed caregivers in our culture and women outlive men by at least seven years, the majority of my illustrations have as protagonists a mother and a daughter.

Molly is 44; her mother, Frances, is 79; her father, Howard, 84. Molly has one sibling, Laurel, who is 49, married, and has three teenaged children. Molly has been married for 17 years and has a son and daughter, 7 and 11. Although Molly's parents live in Arizona from November through April, they spend the rest of the year in a retirement community about 30 minutes from Molly and Laurel. Frances is in excellent health. She drives a car, plays bridge several times a week, tutors children in reading in a nearby junior high school, and occasionally plays a few holes of golf. Howard, on the other hand, has cardiac problems that required bypass surgery. The surgery was fairly successful and although he now has a pacemaker, Howard considers himself healthy enough to do all the things that make his life meaningful. He golfs, gardens, walks, and attends the symphony in nearby Philadelphia when he is so inclined. Every now and then, however, an understandable fear about his heart or pacemaker may seem like a crisis.

If you were to see this group celebrating Mother's Day at a local restaurant, you would admire their apparent good will and politeness. You would be hard pressed to think of them as a family filled with hard feelings, distance, envy, and hostility. Yet, each family member would be counting the remaining minutes of this oppressive, obligatory family occasion.

Molly and her sister Laurel only speak when necessary—on occasions such as Mother's Day or when they are discussing their parents' health-care needs. Molly thinks Laurel is the favorite child, the one who never gets the emergency phone calls from Mom or her bursts of anger and criticism. Their husbands and children know about the hard feelings between the two sisters and play out a charade of closeness whenever the family has to spend time together. Molly can't be alone with her mother without feeling defensive or anxious. She can't stand talking to her mother on the phone for more than 10 minutes, and often does not answer the phone when she expects her mother to call. Molly is upset that her children have to see the troubles in her family. Howard, distressed over the distance between Frances and Molly but frightened to do anything about it, only speaks to Molly when Frances is not home; both father and daughter feel guilt and pain over the triangle their alliance has created. And so it goes, as a family is torn apart by past and present forces that intermingle in a particular way at a particular time, producing disastrous consequences for everyone. But especially for Molly, whose story follows:

> I was a tough kid, I suppose. A rebel all the way. I know I wasn't easy for a mother like mine, who expected me to be perfect. There was a big fence around our property, and I was always climbing over it to see what was on the other side. I would even climb wearing my Sunday-best, black patent-leather Mary Jane shoes, and all that. My mother never really understood me or wanted to. I was always different from my sister. She allowed herself to be molded in my mother's image—a perfect lady, who wore the right clothes, had the right friends, went to college, and married the right man. I chose not to go to college, taking training to become a nurse instead. My mother could never understand my choice of profession and even though over the years I've managed to earn my master's in nursing, she still refuses to give me recognition for making a success of my life in a field I love. Then I married someone Jewish, further adding to her disappointment. She refused to give me the same wedding or wedding gift she gave my sister. Today, though, I have to admit she has grown to respect and like my husband, and my parents were generous with us when he was laid off for several months.
>
> My mother and I always had trouble talking to each other. She never tried to understand me, to really listen to what I had to say. Consequently, our relationship is superficial. I have never been open with her because the few times I tried, I got nowhere. We were able to go along in this way for quite some time. You know, with our polite surfacy relationship. Five years ago when my father became ill, my mother got understandably scared and needed my sister's and

my help. But it was me rather than my sister whom she called nine times out of ten for all kinds of help, like taking Dad to the doctor, doing the marketing, or arranging for some health care at home. When I ask her how come she doesn't call Laurel once in awhile, she tells me it's because I'm a nurse and Laurel is too busy or stressed. Well, Laurel can drive, cook, market, and talk to health-care professionals. You don't need training in nursing for these chores. And incidentally, it is only in this context that Mom gives my nursing training any credit. Credit, yes, but not thanks.

I ran my butt off for my mother, always hoping that perhaps now that she needed me she would change toward me and stop being so critical of me and my life. Well, she is still critical of everything I do, from the way I raise my kids to how my husband and I choose to spend our vacation. And the problems with my sister have gotten worse, as she continually reminds me of what a wonderful daughter Laurel is, but can never extend me the same praise. My father knows how I feel; he admits Mom is partial to Laurel, but he does not want to get involved. I can understand his position, but sometimes I wish he would come to my defense.

Well, last summer my mother and I had a real falling apart. Just as I was going out the door to take my kids to the beach for the day—all packed with a picnic lunch, shovels and pails, surf boards, towels, and bathing suits—my mother called to say my dad was having palpitations and she wanted me to come over right away and drive them to his physician. I reassured her that it's probably not serious, that he's had these episodes before and they turned out to be harmless. I told her I was certain she could pull herself together enough to drive and that if she couldn't, I told her to try Laurel or get a driver. I told her my children and I planned this special day for quite some time and that I could not disappoint them. Believe me, I told her in the kindest way possible how sorry I was. Well, she let me know that after this betrayal of her and my father, she would never speak to me again.

Laurel, of course, drove them to the doctor. Everything turned out to be okay with my dad. But for eight months she refused to speak with me, slamming the phone in my ear whenever I would try to call her. When I tried to reach my dad on his 84th birthday last year, she hung up. Finally he called back to accept my wishes, and we both cried wishing that things would be better. At that time I implored him to convince Mom to talk to me. I remember telling him that for the rest of my life I would suffer if we ended this way.

The winter went by. Laurel and her family went to Arizona for

Christmas. I was not invited and would not have gone, anyway. About a month before I heard you speak, I called my mother on her birthday. My father answered, telling me that she will not talk to me, and it would be best if I let things be as they are. I told him then that if she turns me down this time, I will never call again. Anyway, she consented to hear me. I started our conversation with the following words: Mom I called to wish you a happy birthday and besides, I feel we really need to talk. I can no longer go on this way. I am in too much pain and I would like us to try to be friends. I have a lot of resentments and I'm sure you do too, and if we can rake up some of these old coals, perhaps we might be able to kindle a new closeness between us. I chose my words very carefully, even waxing poetic, as you can see.

I told her I loved her, that I was hurt over the favoritism she showed my sister, that I really wanted her to understand and accept the person I am. Well, she listened for perhaps three minutes. And then the tirade began: poor me, look what you've done to me; how can you accuse me of favoring your sister; you have no respect for your father and me, especially after all we did for you; I've been a better than good mother to you; other daughters do more for their parents. Realizing at that point that she would never change, that she would always be self-centered and selfish, I knew this was the the mother I would have to own. I am ashamed to say she is not the kind of mother I would like to have. The conversation ended with a recitation of how well she was playing bridge and how well she was feeling and looking.

Well, we are back to the old superficial politeness. But I feel better in that I have been honest. I have forgiven her. She is what she is.

I will always do my best for her, but it's different now. My father just went back into the hospital two days ago, and when she called to tell me, I did not immediately jump in with an invitation to have her to dinner. I would have a year ago. I speak with Dad on the phone and will see him tomorrow morning after I get the kids off to school. Oh, and eventually I'll have her over to dinner, but it will be when *I* have the energy for it. I feel terrible over all this and I think I truly feel worse over what's happened between my sister and me. My mother, Laurel, and I are meeting in a few days to make some long-term care plans for my dad, who might be in some real trouble now. I dread this meeting. Whenever the three of us are together, Laurel and my mother always talk to each other, never to me. My mother never even looks at me when she talks to me. Instead she refers to me in the third person, while directing her words to Laurel. I'm happy to say there may yet may be hope for Laurel and me, because yesterday she called to say she thinks Mom has been unfair and she would like us to have lunch before our meeting. So, who knows!

Well, that's my story. It all hurts, but what can I do? I can't sit and wallow in it. If I think too long about all that has happened, I can't deal with it. I wish it could be different between my mother and me but I know it never will, and I have to go on with my own life. I have to pick up the pieces. I sound as if I'm divorced, don't I?

By this time Molly's dark eyes glistened with tears. Of course, it feels like divorce! Loss is loss, whether it is mate or parent; whether its guise is death, divorce, or shattered dream. And when it is the love of a parent that is missing, the child, no matter what his or her age, feels the presence of a big, gaping hole deep inside. As I retell Molly's story, the words of family therapist James Framo ring in my ears: "No one ever gives up the yearning for the love and acceptance of parents.. . . . Children, and adults as well, will forego their own nature in order to save a parent from going crazy or in order to become the kind of person a parent (or parent representative) can love."[5]

Molly, for as long as her parents live, hungers for that kind word of recognition, that gesture of love, that accolade of parental approval, accepting her as she is. Although she will travel well through life without these blessings, she will always wonder what she and her life might have been like with them. Though of sound mind, body, and heart, Molly will have those shaky moments of doubt, when her mother's negative energy surrounds her, causing her to question whether she is, indeed, a lovable human being.

With all of Molly's resentments, grievances, and hurts, it would be easy to write a strong case for Molly's hating her mother. The problem is, Molly does not hate Frances. Able to see both the dark and light sides that make her a whole person, Molly says the following about her mother:

> My Mom is not all bad, you know. I suppose no one really is. Anyway she was a marvelous teacher. She taught junior high school English and history, and her students loved her. She does better with people she is not really close to. Probably closeness scares her. Her students loved her and saw qualities in her my sister and I never knew existed. And I have to believe I've inherited her love-of-peo-

ple qualities. After all, I did become a nurse. My mother is not a cruel person. She has a lot of compassion and in the '60s developed one of the first Head Start programs in our state. I guess she's different within the family. Other people like her—her friends, the people she plays bridge with. As a child, too, our house was always filled with my parents' friends. That was a nice way to grow up.

Impressed so far with Molly's level of maturity, I continued with questions about what she knew of the history of her parents' relationships to their parents. Unable to shed much light on this area because her father's parents died before she was born and her maternal grandparents moved to Florida when she was in her late teens, she told me with an air of almost sudden discovery that her mother was never really faced with the responsiblity of caring for her own parents. As was typical of Irish families of another era, a bachelor uncle lived with Molly's grandparents until they died. "Would it have made a difference for the better," Molly wondered out loud, "if my mother were saddled with parent care when she was middle aged? We can't mend the past but maybe she would at least be more appreciative of all that I do for her now. I suppose I foolishly thought that what would happen is that things would be different for us at this time in our lives."

From conversation about her parents and grandparents to comments about her children was an easy leap for Molly. It took no prodding whatsoever to get her to talk about what she expects from her children when she is old. The last thing Molly wanted was to replicate what was happening with her parents with her own children. In her struggle to figure out what she owes her parents, she asks herself, "What can I rightfully expect from my own children when I am old?" Although she adheres to the conventional wisdom that daughters usually "do more" and feels a heightened sensitivity toward her daughter because of gender identification, Molly hopes that she will not have to depend upon either her son or daughter for too much support when she is old.

Molly is fiercely determined to create an open, honest relationship with her children. She does not hide from her children the current conflicts with her mother, for example. She openly confesses her hurt over this sad state of affairs. She is especially sensitive to her daughter's concerns, discussing with her, when appropriate, how *their* relationship is radically different from the one she had with her mother when she was 12 years old. She reassures her that though they may have natural ups and downs in the future, they will always be emotionally close; they will be able to talk to each other. Molly, furthermore, encourages both her son and daughter to be friendly with their grandparents, emphasizing over and again that her wounded relationship with Frances and Howard need not be theirs; that her mother, especially, has gifts and strong points that shine when she is with other people.

Molly's story reminds me of a wonderful Chinese tale that sums up in a few words this universal dilemma. A son, observes his father in his rocking chair and notes that the old man takes more than he can give, eating the little rice his family grows and unable to do his share of the hard work. He decides to do away with him, devising what he considers a most practical and sensible plan for his disposal. He immediately constructs a wooden box large enough to hold his father, which he will hurl over a cliff. After he places his father in this box and as he wheels him in a wheelbarrow to the precipice, he is surprised to hear a tap, tap on its lid, followed by his father's gentle voice. "Son," his father advises, "I understand why you are doing this, but at least let me give you a helpful suggestion. Why not just throw me over without the box, for one day your children might need it."

Molly and just about every middle-aged child with aging parents who are parents are exquisitely aware that their behavior could easily become the next generation's model for how sons and daughters should behave. This is a perfect reason why they should resolve long-standing conflicts and finish old business while their parents are alive—their own children are watching from the wings to see how it is done.

For solo dancers who are parents themselves, resolving such crises is difficult. Interdependence of the generations, explored in Chapter 2, means everything to them. Molly and those like her, afraid of recycling their troubled relationships into the next generation, know that they must set a good example for their children, who are unconsciously preparing for that time when their own parents are old. Friendship and harmony with the next generation are at stake if some compassionate solutions are not achieved.

For their own sake and for the sake of their children, solo dancers must do two things. First, they must *forgive* their parents for not acknowledging them as adults. And second, they must *grieve* for the loss of a relationship they wanted to have with their parents but could not. Their parents will not be their friends, they will never know their parents' real feelings about growing old and dying, and they will never experience the deep satisfaction of being acknowledged by their parents as dependable children.

Blenkner's plea that children see the person behind the parent is of immeasurable help in the forgiveness process.[6] Seeing their parents as flesh-and-blood, vulnerable human beings, shaped by unique experiences with *their* imperfect parents can bring children considerable comfort. Knowing their parents' anger and inflexibility have as their source wounds from an earlier battleground, they are able to interact with them in a less defensive, more compassionate way.

The words of Henry T. Close bear directly upon the immense chore of forgiveness. He advises us:

> To grow up, it is necessary for you to forgive your parents. But you must forgive them for *your* sake, not theirs. Their self-forgiveness is up to them, and they cannot afford to wait for you to forgive them any more than you can afford to wait for them to forgive you. When you do not forgive them, it means that you are still expecting all your parenting from them. You are clinging to them in the hope that if you can make them feel guilty enough, they will finally come through with enough parenting. But this is impossible, and in order for you to be really free . . . you must forgive.[7]

In addition to being really free, forgiveness ultimately makes it easier for children to care for their elderly parents with compassion. Seeing their aged parents as people, forgiving them their all-too-human imperfections, and accepting them as they are, children are able to "be there" for their parents without choked-up rage. And at the very least, they teach by example to *their* children—the next generation—the range and depth of mature love.

But how does a grown child such as Molly honor a difficult parent like Frances? How can she honor her with grace and compassion when Frances gives back nothing in return? How does Molly use her knowledge of Frances as a limited person and forgive her as long as Frances behaves the way she does? How does Molly keep her self esteem when whatever she does is never good enough for Frances?

There are no standard answers to these questions, all of which are central to the stories I relate about grown children who dance solo. Unless they want to be completely disconnected from their parents—and most do not—grown children must forgive, accept their parents as who they are, do the best they can within their personal limits, and live their lives. Maintaining this attitude is an endless struggle requiring conscious effort. I have no set of instructions how to do it. As Molly did, you simply do it.

The most helpful guidance I can offer comes directly from a client. With a parent as difficult as Molly's, Bob felt he needed something concrete to get him through some of the trying times. As a result, with his wife's help, he drew up a list of affirmations to help him manage his emotions while dealing with his manipulative 78-year-old mother. Whenever Bob feels himself becoming angry and defensive, he refers to these affirmations. He even made a copy on a small card to carry in his wallet. More than willing to share them with others, he hopes they will be a source of strength to them as well.

Affirmations Regarding my Relationship with My Mother

1. I am in charge of and responsible for my own life.
2. My purpose is to *live* my one and only life, to become my best person, to be uniquely me. Doing so is the best way to honor my parents.
3. My first responsibility is to my family. Each of us in our family has a right to her or his own life.
4. My energy will be used positively in my life. This includes time for family, community activies, personal improvement, relaxation, exercise, and the like. I am a good person when I choose to use my energies in these ways.
5. I am separate from my mother and I have my own life. Therefore, I do not need to change her at all. I recognize that much of her parenting behavior actually may be coming from her primitive, wounded "child."
6. I do not know what Mom is feeling—I can only know what she expresses about her feelings, verbally or nonverbally. I am not responsible for her feelings, such as anger, sadness, loss, or embarrassment.

7. I am responsible for my own feelings, thoughts, and actions regarding Mom. She has no control over my feelings, thoughts, and actions. Only I control my feelings, thoughts, and actions.
8. I accept that I may never "get through" to Mom.
9. I am not responsible for Mom's behavior, actions, or problems. I cannot control what Mom says to her family, friends, and other persons.
10. I have a right to let Mom know that negative comments bring me down and I may choose to not listen to them.
11. I recognize that I can never satisfy all of Mom's needs. I have a right to say "no" to anything when I feel I am not ready, it is unsafe, or violates my values.
12. I will be there for Mom when she truly needs me. I can also help Mom by finding other resources for her, such as a counselor, minister to talk with, or other services that may help her meet a need.
13. I have a right to be happy, relaxed, playful, and even frivolous.
14. I can take care of myself, change, and grow.

Lynne, 54, whose 80-year-old widowed mother, Kay, phones her or sees her almost every day, demonstrates how hard it can be to forgive. Unlike Molly, whose parents spend almost half the year away and whose mother, Frances, has a husband who provides companionship, Lynne has little relief from her mother's demands for care and attention. Under such frequent bombardment, forgiveness may not only be difficult, it may be impossible.

Lynne has been my client for three years. She came to see me shortly after her father died because she was having a hard time accepting his death and because her mother's incessant cries for help were interfering with and exacerbating her own. Although Lynne has a sister and brother, they live far enough away to be unavailable for physical support or assistance. Married, with three independent children, one grandchild, and holding a high-level job with a major insurance company, Lynne rarely has a minute to spare for herself. Usually able to cope with her hectic schedule, even enjoying the organizational challenge it presents, she frequently feels she has lost control of her life because of her mother's sudden widowhood.

Like Molly, Lynne credits her mother with many pluses. It is from her mother, she says, that she learned the value of honesty and fairness. It is from her mother that she gained an appreciation of art, opera, good literature, and music. Lynne, who is a better than average watercolorist, says that without her mother's constant encouragement of her artistic abilities, she would not have known the pure enjoyment of spending hours sketching and painting the outdoors she loves so much.

Yet, Lynne's relationship with her mother is haunted by phantoms from the past. Like Molly, she was never the favorite child. It would seem that from time immemorial, elderly parents have unwittingly created sticky sibling problems. Just look at Shakespeare's King Lear. In giving more love, trust, or favors to one child rather than another, parents, besides stirring up jealousies, sometimes make unwise choices. The trusted sibling turns out to be unreliable; the loved one turns out to be undevoted. Frequently too, the hands that feed and care for them are smacked; those that do nothing are stroked. So, whether Molly, Lynne, or Lear's daughter Cordelia, the faithful may be spurned.

Lynne never received credit for her accomplishments, while her siblings did. She could never tell her mother how she really felt because her mother would invalidate her feelings with, "You don't really feel that way!" or "No one would feel that way but you!" or "That doesn't hurt!" or "You're stupid to say such a thing." In the same vein, when Lynne's hair was long, her mother complained it should be short. When she agreed to have it cut, it wasn't cut short enough. When she finally lost weight, she was too thin, and when she regained some, she was too fat. When Lynne married a man who didn't "come from the proper background," Kay treated him badly, either totally ignoring or sarcastically demeaning him. While Lynne's son underwent surgery, Lynne's mother, heartlessly oblivious to Lynne's agony, moaned and groaned about the favored sister's financial woes.

As Lynne tells it, not once in her entire 54 years has her mother ever apologized to her for something she said or did that hurt her daughter. Lynne's own words best sum up her feelings about her mother: "I want her once and for all to grant me the right to be what I want to be. I want her to say she's really sorry about some of the things she has done to me and my family. I want her especially to apologize for the cruel way she treated my husband. For this, I would like to bring her to her knees!"

Lynne tries to forgive, but she cannot. Our counseling sessions, interspersed with glimmers of hopeful progress that are quickly extinguished, are largely marked with frustration as Lynne bristles over each new confrontation or slight offense. Buried resentments may be dug up in a telephone conversation in which Kay criticises Lynne for being too tired to talk when she called the other night about a hearing-aide problem. Or Lynne and Kay might be sailing smoothly when Kay, from nowhere, admonishes Lynne that if she accepts the invitattion to attend the engagement party that her hated sister-in-law is giving for her grandson, she will never speak to Lynne again. Kay's creed seems to be: if you love me you will hate the people I hate. In describing this episode to me, Lynne says Kay ended her diatribe with the following vindictive words: "I hope one day someone will do something to hurt you that you cannot forget or forgive." Not surprisingly, Lynne told me it took all the control she could muster from blurting out, "Someone already has, Mom, and that someone is *you*!"

Reacting to her mother's lectures and painful inuendos in anger and always armed with an instant barb or "I gotcha," Lynne remains an adolescent. The fact she seeks approval from her mother, as Henry Close explains, indicates how strong her need to be parented still is. Lynne is still waiting for those tender strokes and warm words that were denied her throughout her life. And yet, despite her emotional deprivation and its resulting anger, Lynne is there for Kay whenever she requires help or support. Be it shopping, marketing, transportation to the hairdresser or doctor, theater outings, dinners or lunches out, or taking her to visit children and grandchildren in other states, Lynne is ready and able, even if it means using a vacation day. Lynne exclaims, "I'd move heaven and earth for her, but I never get it back. Why can't she give me some recognition! Is that too much to ask!"

As long as Lynne pines for "that something back," the maturity she gropes for will be forever out of her reach. Lynne cannot move into this grown-up role, that last step, until she accepts Kay as the person she is, forgives her, and relates to her not as powerful mom but as equal human being, no better or worse than anyone else.

The tragedy of Lynne's story, however, is that she is afraid to talk to her mother about what pains her. Unlike Molly, who at least is able to speak her heart, to confront her mother with her hurt, Lynne backs off from any encounter that makes her vulnerable. Because past emotional injuries were so devastating, Lynne, quite understandably, will not put herself in a position where she can be squashed: "I can't talk to her about those things (feelings); she would never understand. She never did! It has not been part of our way of living. If I did, she'd get angry, tell me I'm wrong, and I would suffer as I did when I was a child." Lynne finalizes these thoughts with a courageously insightful statement: "I know being afraid of my mother means I am still a child. I know this. Despite my smarts and brilliant career, I remain terrified of her anger and disapproval."

Although Lynne, like Molly, knows little of her mother's life history, she does know one significant piece of information. Scary in what it reveals to Lynne about the perpetuation of family patterns into the next generation, it relates to Kay's behavior toward *her* father in the final years of his life. Kay, who was not the favored child in her family and jealous of the sister who was, in a last-ditch attempt to outdo that sister, obsessively cared for their father until the day he died. Traveling by train almost daily the 35 miles to where her father lived, she cooked for him, kept his house, and performed many other personal tasks that gave him comfort and allowed him to die in his own home. Her father repaid her for this ultimate kindness by changing his will, leaving the few assets he had to Kay rather than her sister. As is common with such last-minute alterations, Kay's sister contested the will, throwing both siblings into a prolonged court battle that not only completely drained their father's legacy but left them enemies for all time.

What heartbreak could be spared, what energy saved, if Lynne can learn from her mother's experience. It warns her to let go, to forgive, to accept, or else her destiny may be like her mother's—perpetual family strife, deep personal anger and resentment, and no inner peace.

Now, whose fault is all this generational tension? Who is responsible for this terrible impasse? Is Lynne to blame more than Kay, or vice-versa? As in all intimate relationships between people, from marriage to friendship to parent-child, there are no clear-cut, simple solutions to the conflicts and predicaments they breed. I could say both are equally to blame. Yet, in the sense that Lynne can't let go of her anger towards Kay, accept her for the fallible adult she is, and forgive her her all-too-human foibles, she bears heavy responsibility for this unhappy situation.

Using the same logic, however, I could just as easily assign blame to Kay. After all, if she could tame her negativity toward Lynne, reign in her craving for parental power, recognize the futility in always having to be right, pull back on her tendency to have the last word, grant appropriate approval of Lynne's kindnesses, and listen non-defensively when Lynne talked about her feelings, she would help her daughter become a mature daughter. Since she cannot do these things, she must share the blame.

Dishing out blame is not what mature relationships are about, however. Blame does not heal, resolve conflicts, produce change, or create new understanding in difficult relationships. In Lynne's case, for example, placing blame will not dim her anger towards her mother, nor will it give her or Molly the parental acknowledgment each desires.

The following story of Josh illustrates both the pointlessness of blame and its power to paralyze parents and children in their efforts to make peace. When Josh ultimately gives up blame for personal responsibility, he reaches a new level of maturity and freedom.

Josh, 50, was one of the few men to attend the Tuesday-night circle, joining because he could not but desperately wanted to forgive his mother. A 15-years-plus member of Alcoholics Anonymous, he was a welcome addition to our gathering because of the ease with which he expressed his feelings. He compelled each of us to be less afraid to speak from the heart, and his honesty and openness sparked the entire group. Josh had much in common with Molly and Lynne. Where he differed from them was in his awareness that his relationship with his parent was beyond reclaiming. What Josh wanted more than anything was to get rid of the ferocious anger he harbored toward his mother, Edith, so that when they had to be together, which, unfortunately, was frequently, he could at least relate to her from compassion rather than anger.

Josh described his relationship with Edith this way:

> My mother and I have always been like this (he locks both hands together in a fist so tight that the knuckles whiten). I don't like my mom; I'm not even sure I love her. And now she is my responsibility

for as long as she remains alive. She just moved into a subsidized senior housing complex about 10 minutes from where my wife (second marriage), my 10-year-old son, and I live. Why she chose to live near me instead of my younger brother who is her favorite, I will never understand. But here she is and she's all mine.

Unlike Molly and Lynne, Josh knows a great deal about his mother's life history and the crucial events that shaped her life. Not only does Edith, 82, enjoy talking about her past to anyone who will listen, but brilliant and articulate, she has written reams and reams about it in essays and personal journals. Josh, in fact, brought to the group some of his mother's autobiographical writings from college, complete with professors' markings and comments, so that we might have a better sense of Edith. As Josh puts it, "My mother's biggest problem is that she really believes she's the greatest person in the world and that everyone wants to know all about her, that they would, indeed, be *honored* to know all about her!"

Painting Edith's life in the broadest strokes possible, she was born in England to a mother who left her in foster care at an early age and to a father whom she never knew. Her story, almost Dickensian in nature, is about the courageous struggles of a bright young girl who rises above her mean existence to a life of culture and respectability. Arriving in the United States at age 11 with an aunt who took her out of foster care, Edith worked hard, saved money to attend college, was an editor for a magazine, had love affairs with men of status, married, and had children. Considering life as mother and wife ordinary and judging herself a superior mortal, Edith pushed her husband, whom she described as someone "without drive and appreciation for beauty," to do and be more, until he eventually deserted her and their sons. Meeting the challenge of survival once again, she found a job that drew upon her literary talents and provided her with the means to feed, clothe, and educate her family.

The feelings one has about Edith while reading her autobiographical materials are ambivalent. On the one hand, it is impossible not to be in awe of this gutsy, resourceful person, who like the phoenix from mythology rises from the rubble of loss and despair not once but many times. Without a shred of self pity or fear and ever confident that she will meet the goals she sets for herself, Edith engages life fully. She is an inspiration to all who are inclined to surrender in the wake of life's twists and turns. I wept, laughed, and applauded her adventures, all the time thinking what a wonderfully exciting and interesting person she would be to know.

To know her as an *acquaintance*, yes, or perhaps even a friend might be fun. To know her as mother as Josh does, however, could be hell. For the darker side of Edith is composed of her pompousness, her strong feelings of entitlement, her inclination towards control, and her condescension to those who do not share her values or measure up intellectually. Considering Edith then in her rich entirety, as a mother she would be "difficult," as an elderly mother, impossible.

At 82, with a hip replacement, a pacemaker, and moderate vision problems, still every bit the crusty warrior, Edith has come to live near her son, Josh. It requires little imagination to envision what Edith is like at this time. No longer in full command of her world and dependent upon Josh and his wife to help her with the marketing and shopping, to drive her to doctors' appointments, and to provide her with some sort of social network, Edith's life is topsy-turvy. High command having slipped from her grasp, she is unable to cope with her losses, to allow interdependence with others, or to find meaning in her life as it has evolved.

She complains to Josh constantly: his son shouldn't be so abrupt with her over the telephone; his wife forgot to make a hairdresser appointment; Josh hasn't played gin rummy with her in a week; he spends more time with his family than with her; he brings home the wrong can of tuna fish; he was late getting her to church. Her range of grievances is broad and unending as she tries to fashion some control from her role as parent. She goes so far as to threaten Josh that unless he is more respectful of her wishes, she will leave him out of her will. Indeed, Josh's inheritance teeters on every flare-up and Edith's mood at the time.

One evening when Josh has a barbecue for friends, he uneasily decides to invite Edith. She not only scolds him like a child in front of his guests but reveals to everyone that he is a member of Alcoholics Anonymous. It was this final act of humiliation and betrayal that prompted him to come for help.

What can be done to help Josh feel less angry toward Edith? Is there any way to lessen the acrimony that defines their relationship? Or are they so mired in ancient hurts and recriminations that they are beyond healing? Given Edith's resistance to change—to talk, to compromise, to let go of power—and her need to intimidate to attain control, what is left for Josh? "Why should I take responsibility," Josh asks me, "when my mother is clearly to blame for this mess? Why must the onus fall on me? Let her do some work and bend a little!" What Josh fails to understand is that he cannot play either waiting or tit-for-tat games with his mother. Whether Edith does her share of the giving or makes the first move toward settling things does not matter. Change—and with it, hope—lies in Josh taking responsibility for his own life.

Family theory teaches us that when an interaction between two people is "circular" rather than "linear," blame cannot be pinpointed. This concept applies to Josh and Edith: Edith's behavior sparks a certain response in Josh that in turn fuels Edith's anger. This in turn causes Edith to attack again, which in turn provokes Josh again to respond in kind. And so it goes, to use the words of family therapist Donald S. Williamson, with "the buck in constant circulation." Dr. Williamson, in looking at circularity, wonders, "If responsibility is nowhere—then where can we look for change."[8]

If we consider Josh's original description of his relationship with his mother as two hands locked tightly together in a sort of double fist, then Josh's task becomes even more clear-cut. If he chooses, Josh has it within his power to free his hand from his mother's hold, thereby changing the nature of their pattern of relating to one another. Although he can't change Edith, he can change how he perceives her and experiences their relationship. In other words, should Josh let go of her hand, he would no longer be able to say, "My mother and I are like *this*." What he could say, however, is, "Although my mother is a tyrant, I understand where she's coming from and I no longer need to strike back whenever she pushes my buttons."

When Josh decides to assume responsibility, the battle for control with his mother ends and his relationship with her becomes open to change. No longer vulnerable to her intimidation, no longer blaming her for his predicament, and no longer locked into the tight fist, he feels less helpless and more adult. He achieves a certain peace with himself, if not with Edith. At this point, Josh is taking charge of himself and his life.

To quote Williamson again, "In the final resort it (family theory) holds the individual accountable for the movie playing in his head by day and the reruns by night. It is my contention that the ending of intergenerational intimidation is the royal road to personal authority in life; and personal authority is the source of personal responsibility, including responsibility for change."[9]

Grown up, dependable, able to see Edith as a person, and forgiving her, Josh, though not mature as a son, feels better about himself and is certainly less helpless. Although, like Molly, Josh remains stalled—near, but not quite at the top of the ladder to adulthood—the blame and adolescent anger he carried for so long have evaporated. Josh is okay now. He cares for Edith with equanimity and charity not possible before he became personally responsible for his actions.

Is personal responsibility a perfect solution? No, because there are no perfect solutions when it comes to intimate human relationships. Does self-change have the power to change parents? The answer is "perhaps."

The following story of Jane and her mother takes us into the realm of "perhaps." Jane, who came to see me because she was at wit's end over her mother's inability to listen to her, decided there must be a way to make things better in their relationship.

"Talking to her is like talking to the wind," says Jane of her many conversations with her mother. "She doesn't want to hear that I am tired when she calls after I return from work. She doesn't want to hear that I haven't called for a few days because I am busy and not because I don't love her. She doesn't understand how much Ben and I want and need to be alone in the beach house we rent for two weeks every summer. The first summer we invited Mom to join us for a few days was a disaster. She was depressed, needed lots of attention, and wasn't satisfied with the shortness of the visit. We squandered our time together in fighting rather than in getting closer. I really love my mother, but everything I say or do she takes as a personal affront. If I can't have her to dinner one weekend because I happen to be tired, she thinks it's because I don't enjoy her company. I always feel defensive with her. At this point I do the best I can to avoid her. Either I have my answering machine on or do not answer the phone at all when she calls. When my father was alive she was different. I know how lonely she is, but she can be warm and charming when she wants to, and the few friends who know her well have seen this side."

Jane was a client after my own heart. Psychologically oriented and unafraid to take a good look at herself, she was a pleasure to work with. For a year we explored her fears of hurting her mother's feelings, her childlike powerlessness in her mother's presence, and her guilt over expressing her needs.

In time, Jane stopped avoiding her mother and, instead, each time they spoke on the phone or were together she firmly asserted herself. When she was too tired for a long telephone conversation, for example, she spoke up; when her mother heaped on guilt with "you just don't care about me" statements, she calmly said "not so," and suggested they change the subject to something pleasant. She resolutely continued on this course, despite what appeared to be her mother's stonewalling and deafness to her requests. Because Jane never gave up on her efforts at being adult, being adult became more comfortable. Her language became less harsh, its tone more tender, her responses less studied and more spontaneous. All the time she was talking, stating her position, and making her point, Jane persevered upon her path.

In time, the relationship itself appeared different to Jane. What she once described as a bitter, no-win contest with her mother was now characterized by the terms "irksome," "sad," or "unfortunate." The relationship had changed because Jane had changed. She was now handling things, she was no longer defensive, and she had taken responsibility for her own behavior. Maybe it was paying off because now and then Jane thought she detected in her mother a glimmer of accommodation. And one day when Jane came in for her session, I could tell by the ease with which she fell into my chair that something had happened.

Jane had taken her mother to the theater to celebrate her 75th birthday and for the first time in years, they had a wonderful time with each other. Describing this glorious day as a "turning point" in their relationship, Jane spent the entire hour recounting all the details.

> I think that a separation has occurred between me and my mother. I am learning that she will never change, but I am more accepting of that fact now. The intellectual awareness of how she will react or what she will say prepares me for my responses and feelings

toward her. I do not get as riled up or impatient with her "foibles" (my perception) and what irks me about her. I think about a potential problem situation before I actually do anything about it.

We had a wonderful day in New York recently. I took her to see a play. It was a beautiful day in all ways, and my mother was most appreciative. We had a delicious lunch at a delightful little French cafe near the theater (her choice) and she loved the play (both laughter and teary-eyed emotions showed). She periodically gave me spontaneous hugs and kisses and expressed openly what a wonderful time she was having.

Maybe it was her open appreciation of this day with her recently expressed appreciation of "You're such a good daughter; you do so much for me," but, I think I have reached a kind of turning point, even epiphany, in my relationship with Mom. I have more compassion and empathy for her aloneness and a better understanding of why she is the way she is. I have a deeper desire to please her, not in a submissive way, but to help make her final years more peaceful and happy. To please her, not at the expense of myself, but to bend a little more and to try a little harder so that she will know that I do love her and do care for her and that I want us to reach a resolution or meeting of the minds in our relationship. This seems a small price to pay for my peacefulness.

I think I'm actually realizing now that my mother won't be here forever and that I want our relationship to be one of tranquility, rather than angst or strife. I can project to the time when my mother will no longer be around and sense the emptiness I will feel.

I want to remember the "coming together" rather than the "pulling apart" facets of the relationship. I want my feelings (and hers) to be compatible and harmonious; I want a caring relationship between Mother and Daughter.

I think I'm on the right road to this relationship.

Jane is on the right road. Her willingness to change sparked change in her mother, who was then able to grant Jane the "good daughter" recognition she deserved. As Jane became mature and her mother wiser, *both* came together as equal human beings, as friends, respectful of each other's individuality.

As it turned out, Jane's thoughts about her mother's death were prophetic. Five months later, quite unexpectedly, the prolonged stomach pains her mother experienced were diagnosed as advanced pancreatic cancer. Within three weeks she was dead. Jane's mother knew she was dying and during her brief hospital stay, she and Jane were able to fully complete their "coming together." They shared what each meant to the other and they reminisced about family, Jane's sister, grandchildren, and sons-in-law: Her mother was able to tell Jane when she wanted to just close her eyes and when she wanted to have company, she discussed funeral and financial arrangements with Jane, and she was able to express anger and exasperation to Jane over how childishly evasive some of her doctors were. "I know I am dying," she would say to Jane. "I would have to be a fool to believe their lies about my condition." Jane was with her mother constantly, feeding her ice cream, holding her hand, stroking her head, combing her hair, and eventually holding her as she died. She even delivered the eulogy at her mother's funeral. And although some of the pulling-apart facets of their relationship will painfully tug at Jane from time to time for as long as she lives, she will always have the inner peace of knowing she and her mother finished their lives together as friends.

For those who cannot succeed as Jane did, hope, nevertheless, prevails. First of all, if sons and daughters fail to reach a mature relationship with their parents, it does not mean that they will age with as little wisdom as their parents. Because they have learned from their parents about the high cost of being rigid, the relationship they have with their own children will be based on resiliency and trust. Furthermore, their parents may not have a clue about how to do it right, but there are more than enough elders (and their numbers are growing) out there to serve as role models. Once children forgive, they are free to find other parenting from people who are willing to open their arms in friendship and love.

This is why a 55-year-old high school mathematics teacher whose mother had let her down again and again with a string of broken promises, is able to say, "I've always had surrogates in my life and have had no trouble finding them. They've given me the trust, love, warmth, approval, and understanding that was never my mother's particular talent. I've had therapy, which has helped. I can't say it hasn't been a struggle, because it has. But it's all been worth it. I feel full and blessed and have raised two wonderful children who are my friends."

I am, at this point, reminded of a poignant story told me by a colleague about one of her clients. Reminiscent of the theme in the 1992 film, *Fried Green Tomatoes*, it concerns a 43-year-old man who formed a loving filial relationship with a 78-year-old woman with whom he became acquainted through mutual business interests. Having come to terms with his own emotionally limited parents in that he accepted them as persons and forgave them their abuse, he, nevertheless, longed for the nurturing parent he never had. Finding what he needed in this remarkably grown up and emotionally generous woman, he became her caregiver and surrogate son. When she became seriously ill, needing additional help, he found an apartment for her near his own home so that he and his wife could be available if an emergency occurred. She acknowledged the love, affection, and physical support he gave her every day; whether by telling him outright, writing a note, or warmly hugging or caressing his hand, she thanked him with full heart until the moment she died. From her he not only received the affirmation his own parents could not give, he learned more than books can teach about what it is to grow old, become dependent, and die with grace. Through his relationship with her, he completed the stage of filial development denied him by his own parents.

Children who have troubled relationships with their parents do not necessarily have them with their own offspring. Such children who have come to me for help, because of their personal struggles generally go out of their way to be devoted and sensitive parents, grandparents, and friends. As parents, they are especially determined to do better by their own children. What they dread more than anything is a replica of the relationship they had with their parents.

I want to stress that such children have the precious, final opportunity to short-circuit the flow of one generation's sins to the next. By taking responsibility for their own actions and their own lives, unlike their parents, they guarantee a different destiny for their own children. Best of all, in showing their offspring the way, the filial maturity that eluded them as middle-aged children comes back to them in a different form, when as elderly parents they can graciously accept *their* children's care, while teaching them how to age with purpose.

What Do We Owe?

My friend, 60, divorced, and recovering from a mastectomy calls with piercing urgency in her voice. She wants to talk about her mother, who has just turned 88. "Mother is doing fine," my friend says, "but of late, I've noticed her gait is slower, her hands tremble more, her appetite is poor. I think she's going down hill fast and I don't know what to do. I love her more than I can tell you! She has been a good mother; I can't imagine a day without her. She will soon need me and I don't know how much I can give to her. I feel I owe her so much. But my own life is so complicated. I'm unprepared for all this and confused. I don't know what is required of me."

What my friend is searching for are some answers to the question of "owing." She is not alone in her quandary. Because of increased longevity and the remarkable changes in lifestyle brought on by technological advances, the question of who owes whom what and how much must be looked at anew.

Honoring our elderly mothers and fathers in Biblical times or even at the turn of this century was a dramatically different process than it is today. The Commandment to honor thy father and mother no longer rings as clear as it once did. Creating more confusion than clarity in an urbanized society where parents and children are thrown into separate and busy orbits, it requires new definition and interpretation. For despite the jarring effects of industrialization on the way we live, parents and children need each other as much as ever. And when parents become old, requiring certain supports and assistance from their offspring, their children do not let them down. Their children "honor" them.

The fact that the parent-child bond has endured throughout this modern chaos testifies to the strength of the ties that bind the generations together. It also demands that we do all we possibly can to keep those ties viable. Although it is hard to describe the nature of this bond, we can say that it is powerful, precious, and complex.

Although the old order changes, requiring that parents, children, and grandchildren find new ways to love, to negotiate conflicts, to talk, and to care for each other, the affection and devotion that flow between the generations remain constant. Parents and children still count upon each other to "be there," to take each other in, to open their arms and hearts when times are hard and no one else seems to understand. These things do not change. They are good and wholesome, their essence is life-affirming, and they must be sustained and nourished.

A 1989 Gallup Poll, *The Family in America*, tells us in numbers and statistics about the quality of parent-child relationships today. Contrary to popular fears, the American family is not in danger of demise. The poll's author, Larry Hugick, writes, "People enjoy being with their family members and wish they had more time to spend with them." Despite a transient population, "Most adult children live within one hour's driving distance of a parent. . . . and continue to stay in touch with their extended families over the course of their lifetimes." Indeed, latest statistics show that about 13 percent of older noninstitutionalized people live with children, siblings, or other relatives. "The percentage of older people living with their children increases with age: 14 percent of the men and 26 percent of the women over 85 years of age live with one of their children." As the twenty-first century approaches, two things are certain: (1) the number of old people will increase and (2) families, though shrinking in size, will continue to give the bulk of care to their elderly parents.[1]

In their compelling book, *The Work and Family Revolution*, Barbara S. Vanderkolk and Ardis A. Young tell us we are entering a new age where family values are regaining importance.[2] The emphasis on work and money that pervaded the 80s is giving way to more human and humane considerations. Younger people in the workforce who have children and their middle-aged counterparts who are caring for elderly parents want to achieve a better balance of work and family. Responding to the needs of this group, companies such as Stride-Rite in Massachusetts and St. Francis's Extended Health Care in Washington state have established intergenerational day-care centers. Procter & Gamble, Merck, and DuPont, to name but a few, are other companies that not only pay attention to family matters but have instituted strong programs that benefit families. Although "the focus may be on child care now," says Robert Beck, executive vice-president for Corporate Human Resources at Bank of America, ". . . eldercare will become the critical issue of the future."[3]

The birth rate declines; the number of elderly is on the rise. Yet, if this is the future trend, how is it we, as a society, are so ill-informed about the needs of those who are aged and their families? While much is written about what to do and how to do it in the earlier years of the family when parents are raising their children, the body of practical knowledge about the later years, though increasing, remains slim. The "how-to" shelves of book stores reflect this discrepancy. Loaded with hundreds of books on every facet of child rearing, they lack sufficient information for those of us who are lost in the wilderness of the filial crisis years.

Since knowledge helps us make informed decisions, and considering the fact that we spend more years with our parents as adults than we do as children, additional emphasis must be placed on intergenerational relationships in the later years. This does not diminish the importance of the early stages of family life. Nor is it meant to pit one generation against the other in unwholesome competition. To have healthy relationships with our families, we must have information about all phases of the life cycle.

As I noted in the preceding chapter when talking about Dr. Margaret Blenkner, the final stage of filial maturity as a stage unto itself, "cannot be wholly described in terms of earlier behavior or earlier influences."[4] As a stage that is becoming, it must be understood on its own, with its own unique dynamics and characteristics.

My dismay over the lack of educational material on this subject does not suggest there is any similarity between relating to the elderly and relating to young children. I am always cautious when these two stages might be compared. Roles do not reverse. Maturity, reciprocity, and respect form the bedrock of parent-child relationships in the later years. Although aged parents frequently are as helpless as children, when they are of sound mind and able to determine their destiny—and even when they are not—that helplessness requires a different mode of response.

So, what guidelines are there to help my friend figure out what she owes her mother? What *do* children owe their parents for giving them so much attention, energy, care, love, and devotion? Are words enough for the unending work and sacrifice that go into preparing a child for independence? Is it any wonder that sometimes we think we own them? Is it any wonder that sometimes we expect repayment? Happily, most parents, are healthy enough to let go, to abide by the wise words of Kahlil Gibran in his book, *The Prophet*:[5]

> Your children are not your children.
> They are the sons and daughters of Life's
> longing for itself.
> They come through you but not from you,
> And though they are with you yet they belong
> not to you.
> You may give them your love but not your thoughts.
> For they have their own thoughts.
> You may house their bodies but not their souls.
> For their souls dwell in the house of tomorrow
> which you cannot visit, not even in your dreams.
> You may strive to be like them, but seek not to make
> them like you.
> For life goes not backward nor tarries with
> yesterday.
> You are the bows from which your children as
> living arrows are sent forth.
> The archer sees the mark upon the path of the
> infinite, and He bends you with His might that
> His arrows may go swift and far.
> Let your bending in the archer's hand be for
> gladness;
> For even as he loves the arrow that flies, so
> He loves also the bow that is stable.

And yet, even those parents who know in their hearts that they must give their children wings, feel their children owe them something when they are old. There is a mysterious tug deep down inside us that cries for a little more. A little more of what, we are not sure. As parents, we know we do not want to be a burden, asking too much from children who are busy raising their own children and living their own lives. But we want to know we matter; that our children care. This tension between messages from the heart and head make for uncertainty in word and action, that cause parents to feel abandoned, even though in all likelihood, they are not.

Certain themes resonate in the answers grown-up, mature parents give when I ask them, "What do your children owe you?" Although at first most respond "nothing" or "really very little," a few words down the line "nothing" may become either "well, of course, respect and love" or "I want to know my children care." For an 80-year-old father, "I want to know my children care" translates into, "My children came all the way from California to be with me when I had surgery. They were there when I opened my eyes in the recovery room. This is what means the world to me, and I suppose this is what I expect." For another parent, in her 70s, in good health, and whose children live nearby, "I want to know my children care" means, "We celebrate holidays together and I know they're there for me in a pinch. What more can I expect? They have their own lives to live." For married parents in their early 80s, it was the following lengthier answer:

> They owe us nothing but to live out their own lives as happily as they can. Of course, we want to share family occasions with them and we also appreciate telephone calls; we hesitate to call them too often because they are so busy. The bottom line is we know if there's a problem, we can count on them to be there, to help out. Otherwise we don't expect more than that. After all, they didn't ask to be brought into this world; we made that decision. Thank God, too, we have the financial wherewithal to care for ourselves. If we didn't, I suppose we'd have to ask for help, but we know they would come through.

In summing up the essence of "respect and love," a widowed mother in her early 80s, Tessie, made the following remarks:

> One of my daughters calls me every day, no matter where she is, and that can be as far away as Florida or Paris. I don't ask her to do this; she wants to. That's her way of telling me she loves me. My

other daughter, who lives in the same town as I, calls me whenever she can, and that's alright too. This daughter's life is different. Because she cannot call as often doesn't make her a worse daughter. Both, though, respect my feelings and needs. I lost two husbands and they were there with me through these ordeals. I couldn't have better children. I don't expect more than what they can give and maybe that's why they give me so much.

My dear friends, Mary and Elmira, one in her early 80s, the other in her middle 70s, both widowed, in good health, and with six children and numerous grown grandchildren between them, gave considerable thought to the issue of "owing." Their combined response went like this:

> Maybe we really don't expect enough. After thinking about it, we feel we should expect more. But we have wonderful relationships with our children; we feel so warmly toward them. Really this is all we want. Right now, we are blessed with good health and vitality. But even though all but two of our children live far away, we know if we needed them they would be there to make whatever arrangements were necessary. We feel our children are our friends. When they visit, we have so much to share and talk about. It's really quite marvelous to have reached this stage in our lives when we can be together as equals.

Elmira said specifically of her relationship with her children: "Having been an only child of a dependent mother who became widowed at a young age, I early on decided to emancipate my children. I know from experience what it is like to be bound to a parent who is possessive and needs so very much from children. I made a conscious effort to be different from my mother. Maybe I expect too little, but I don't think so. My children feel free to live their own lives, but at the same time I feel deeply connected to them and I know that feeling is mutual."

She went on to say this about her older son, John, who lives at a distance and whom she sees infrequently: "He's quite involved in his own life, and I understand and accept this. I don't push for more contact and just love the funny notes and drawings he sends me every month. My only regret about our relationship is that I don't know him better. He's such an interesting man and before I move on, I would like to pick his brain. I feel I could learn so much from him. Maybe I'll reach out to him at some point, but however he responds will be alright."

While acknowledging the importance of children living their own lives, it is clear parents also ask that their children stay in touch; that emotionally, they do not keep their distance. Don't forget us; we want to know that we matter; we want to be with your families; we want to know we can count on you in a crisis, are the underlying messages that define what parents expect from their children. The call, over and again, is for affection and dependability rather than concrete or physical assistance. Although parents do not rule out the latter, and many times their children must provide this form of help, they generally hope they will be able to provide these supports for themselves. It is the "being with" more than the "doing for" that parents wish.

Although most parents to whom I speak feel they deserve a certain respect as parents, they feel they are owed this respect because they have been "good" parents. The majority of parents whom I have counseled, known, and spoken to tell me that respect is an earned prize, not an automatic accompaniment to parenthood. Parents who have been uncaring, selfish, or emotionally withholding cannot expect respect from their children.

There seems to be a fine line, however, between what some parents feel they are due as a result of their rearing role and what is due them simply as people. One 78-year-old mother puts it this way: "For my sons' birthdays, I always give them cash. Well, they don't call to say thank you, and I feel this is wrong. Thank you is due me as their parent, but even more so as a human being." And then unwittingly verifying the existence of the fine line, she reverses the equation by adding, "People shouldn't treat people this way, but especially a parent."

In the same vein, parents speak of their objections to a child's angry outbursts or abrasiveness. Said one octogenarian father, "I get angry when my daughter is sarcastic with me about something I've said or done. I know I'm not perfect but she doesn't have to mock or belittle me." Or said another parent of her son, "I don't feel my son has the right to scream and yell at me. At my age and as his parent, I don't have to take that. It's not right. I know I can be overly critical and sometimes I do not mind my business, but I deserve some respect." What about as a *person*, I ask of the latter parent. Does he not owe you respect and decency simply as a human being? "Yes," was the instant answer. But after a brief pause, she added, "As a parent I feel I deserve a little more. Is this wrong of me?"

What these answers point to is the sense of a kind of benign entitlement parents feel in relation to their children. I say "benign," because though parents may sound abusive in response to what they see as "disrespectful" behaviors by their sons and daughters, what they actually ask for is not so terribly much. They do not want their children to give up their lives for them or to become ill while caring for them. They neither expect nor want their children to return to them the total care they gave their children when they were little (see Chapter 3). In fact, they tell you outright they want their children to have it better than they did. What they do hold fast to is the notion they are owed that intangible, elemental something that is forged in the earliest years of child rearing. Call it "respect," "regard," or "honor," it is that extra dimension that is central to the parent-child relationship and distinguishes it from all others. Simply put, blood carries certain demands or obligations. Consequently, as parents *and* as children we experience one another differently from those to whom we are tied by "water," so to speak. To say we expect "nothing" denies the feelings of the heart. For if we have been good or good enough parents, we hurt deep inside if our children do not come through with the affection, the kindness, the attention, the interest, the care. Is it wrong to expect this kind of respect or regard? I don't think so.

There is no uniform way to demonstrate or express affection and love. Wise parents understand their children cannot all be the same. They take into account their differences in personality, their capacity to give, the nature of their lives, and their relationships with them. Nor do they ask that the emotional attention be constant. Tessie does not expect one daughter to call as often as the other. Elmira's son, John, who sends monthly notes with funny drawings, is not pushed to do more. For my friend, Jo, whose 95-year-old mother lives in Utah, her two two-week visits each year are unconditionally welcomed.

I have said that, "Healthy elderly parents, like all healthy people, want to be part of—not outside of—a network of caring, loving persons. What aging parents fear most is isolation from the bustle of family life and activity. Grown children can give their parents this valuable connection."[6] Now, I will add that there are as many ways to deliver this connection as there are parents, children, values, and families. In the final analysis, what matters is that the connection is created and sustained.

In their fervor to be part of family life, some parents leave home and old friends to live near their children and grandchildren. While this usually works for parents and children who thoroughly explore the matter together, for others the decision brings only disappointment. Parents who found it to be a mistake admit that if they had to do it over again they would have stayed home. Mature, sensitive, and loving parents tell me with heavy hearts how they had mistakenly counted on their children to replace their friends. They add how lonely they are in a strange place where every face is also strange. Children tell me how guilty they feel because they cannot fill their parents' loneliness and how resentful they become because they sacrifice this interest or that activity to meet their parents' socialization needs. An especially sad story concerned a couple in their middle 70s who, after having moved to be near their son and daughter-in-law learned a year later that their son was being transferred to another area. My advice to parents who wish to move near their children is first, to clarify expectations and second, find a retirement community nearby if possible, where they can be near their peers. This way, they can enjoy the best of both worlds—the comradery of friends *and* the affection and friendship of their adult children.

Parents generally do not want to be in a position where they have to depend upon their children to provide them with interest and stimulation. They want to entertain themselves—to do as much as they can for themselves as long as possible. Most elderly people are survivors and copers who have lived as long as they have precisely because of their adaptability and resiliency. Although sincere empathy from children brings deep comfort, parents know their journey through old age and eventually to death is one they travel alone; they know their children can understand just so much. A grown child ought to validate a parent's loss with a supportive statement such as, Oh, Dad, I remember how every morning you would enjoy walking to the store for your newspaper and I know how terrible it must be for you now to be unable to do it, but the child will not taste the bitterness of this kind of loss until he himself is old.

Although mature elderly parents want nothing more than their offspring's happiness, sometimes grown children can have severe-enough problems to make such a goal unattainable. Whether their children's trials are marital, family, or financial difficulties, or a grown child's inability to settle down and be responsible, they cause parents considerable anguish. Many parents not only ache for their children's bad luck but also feel resentment over still being on the hook.

Diane said the following of her 44-year-old son, who is now on his third marriage.

> I thought it would be over by now. I never know what to expect next. He has five children, needs my financial help, and still behaves like the child he was and I suppose will always be. I would like not to have to worry about him any more and finally have a clear head. I'm 76, and I deserve a break. What's worse is that he and his older brother do not get along. My older son, who is a successful professional with different values and lifestyle, looks with disdain upon his younger brother. His attitude only adds to my pain. Whenever we all get together for a family affair, my two sons are only coldly polite to each other.
>
> You cannot imagine what it feels like at my age to have to still worry about a child. You know, I call my son every week just to find out if he's okay. Since he doesn't call me to find out how I am, which is as it should be, I call him. When I call my heart is in my mouth. I never know what I will hear—he missed time at work, he was in a car accident, his children from one wife are now living with him, another one left him to live with her, and so it goes. Constant heartache, that's what it is. Therapists have told me to let go already and not make myself so miserable, as there's nothing I can do about it. But believe me it's not that easy. I keep asking myself what I did wrong.

My father has an old saying: "When children are young, they don't let you sleep; when they are old, they don't let you live." Although he and I like to toss this maxim back and forth, with my insisting that when *parents* are old they don't let their *children* live, for Diane and other mothers and fathers his interpretation represents reality. Just as grown children treasure the much-anticipated years of mid-life, parents also look forward to those years when responsibility for and incessant worry over their children is finally at an end. Mature, emotionally healthy parents are more than happy to surrender the pervasive, vigilant guardianship that defines the early years of child rearing. Having given their chidren both roots and wings, they relax with a sigh of relief when the tv blares, "It's 10 o'clock. Do you know where your children are?" The dire warning no longer applies to them.

When this moratorium is not possible, for whatever reason, when elderly parents still must be rock and support for a child, as with Marie and her daughter Roseanne in Chapter 3, parents feel cheated. It is not the natural order of life for parents to remain parents in this all-encompassing, emotionally and physically draining way. Of course, parents always worry. And this is okay. Elmira and Mary, for example, still worry about their children, who are in their 50s. Harry Truman wrote to his daughter Margaret when she was an adult to "call your momma and dad every time you arrive in a town. . . ."[7] A woman I know in her early 90s, who lives alone and whose mind is razor sharp, agonizes over her son's open-heart surgery and the effects it will have on his family. Such ongoing concern goes with the terrain of parenthood. Sooner or later, most parents understand that from the minute they choose to have children, they are never quite free of those unsettling thoughts and feelings over whether their children are okay.

Without diminishing Diane's problems, the special pain of parents whose children are emotionally or physically disabled deserves mention. At 60, 70, or 80 years of age, frequently ill themselves or with waning stamina, these parents have never known a break from the rigors of parenthood. They truly have always been parents whose primary goals are nurturing, protecting and sheltering their children.

Cassandra Ross, director of the Family Support Program for the state of New Jersey, once talked to me of the plight of parents who, now old, can no longer bathe, dress, lift, or give other personal care to their physically disabled children. With deep emotion, she spoke of how these parents "age and fall apart more quickly than their peers" because of their lifetime of constant hard physical work and emotional stress. New Jersey, she said with pride, is giving high priority to personal care services for elderly parents who are caregivers for live-in disabled children.

These services bring needed relief to some parents, but they do not comfort parents whose children suffer chronic mental problems and for whom living at home is impossible. My client Millie, 75, illustrates this special brand of pain. Her 36-year-old schizophrenic son, Joe, has not been home in three years. Roaming the country aimlessly, occasionally stopping at a mental health clinic for medication but more often spending the night in jail or a shelter for the homeless, Joe is a troubled person. Though vitally involved with people and interests and presenting a cheerful image to the world, Millie sobs in my office over what has happened. In trying to understand her fate, asking "Why me?" and then "Why not me?" she carries on her back a burden that can only be genuinely grasped by parents with similar problems. Her fears for Joe's future, not to mention her anxiety over whether she will see Joe again before she dies, pain her deeply.

The affection, the closeness, the warm give and take elderly parents want and need from their children are denied to Millie and Diane. The validation that "the difficult and uncharted task of parenting was fairly successful," that Dr. Headley speaks of in Chapter 4, also eludes them. Their children's troubled lives are usually not intentionally their fault and they would give anything to rectify a situation they know is unchangeable. They are, nevertheless, haunted by the feeling that somehow they could have done something differently or better. While their friends proudly speak of all the ways their *dependable* children help out, they ache over the loss of an experience they will never have. For such parents, the question, What do my children owe me? is only an academic exercise.

Although the tasks of middle age and old age differ, they converge in one important respect.[8] Illuminating what children expect from parents, they tell us something that is at once surprising and yet unremarkable. Both generations really want the same thing— the deep affection and warmth only family and friends can provide. At this stage of life for elderly parents and their middle-aged children, when the years ahead are generally fewer than those already lived, the rewards of human intimacy become increasingly important. Although children in mid-life may still be grasping at opportunities for success in their job, they are beginning to appreciate that there is more to life than material comforts. When they realize that loving relationships make existence worthwhile and create genuine happiness, they are on the same plane of awareness as their aged parents.

Slanting my father's maxim only tells half the story—of course, grown children expect parents to let them live their own lives. But the issue is much larger. Because children in mid-life have the same need for emotional connection as their parents, let us turn to the nature of those needs and the way children communicate them to their aged parents. Because the phrase "to live their own lives" can be misunderstood to mean complete physical and emotional independence from parental ties, it demands more precise definition.

As I noted in Chapter 2, the goal is not independence of child from parent but interdependence of both generations. The conventional theory of separation-individuation, suggesting children must separate from parents to grow up, is untrue and destructive. It is untrue because the emotionally healthy attachment of child to parent is a positive outgrowth of adulthood, not a deficiency. It is destructive because adhering to the notion weakens the parent-child connection at a time when both generations want closeness.

Perhaps the reason why the concept of independence hangs on is what Harvard psychologist Emily Hancock suggests. With a feminist slant that makes general good sense, she wisely (not politically) notes: "The one official map we use to chart collective human progress portrays the journey of the solitary male; independence is the destination toward which he travels singly. Setting oneself apart from others has become an end in itself rather than the pivot between the dependence of childhood and the intimate commitment of adulthood. . . . "[9]

Hancock's "imtimate commitment of adulthood" does not rule out healthy relationships with parents, it includes them. As the primary tie that binds and through which we not only transmit our particular heritage but learn who we are, the parent-child connection sustains us in ways other relationships cannot. To sacrifice this precious attachment would be a tragic error. As I said in the preceding chapter, completing the final task of adulthood for middle-aged children—achieving filial maturity—is impossible without an appropriately intimate relationship between parent and child.

Children raised in relatively functional families do not want to cut themselves off from their aged parents. To the contrary, they want an abiding relationship with them that while emotionally close, reflects and preserves their autonomy as adults. No longer dependent children, they essentially ask for a connection where the old parent-child boundaries are replaced by new ones geared to appropriate privacy and separation. Such boundaries, indistinguishable from those in mature relationships between peers, confirm adulthood for children.

The "appropriate intimacy" I speak of is both the cause and effect of these boundaries.

I hasten to add that children's needs for autonomy and privacy run as deep as those of their parents. Grown-up parents try to keep a healthy distance from their children. This way, they maintain their independence, keep from becoming a burden, and sustain their identity as whole human beings.

Like their parents, grown children also ask for respect for their values, beliefs, needs, and lifestyles. Living, thinking, and doing things dramatically differently from previous generations, they cope with stresses and responsibilities that their parents can barely understand. They do not unrealistically expect their parents to understand the complexity of what their lives are like; if some parents do, their empathy is a welcome bonus. Nor do they ask for their approval or agreement. What they wish is respect as different but equal adults and the ability to negotiate tensions and conflicts on the basis of this equality.

Greg, a 42-year-old divorced father with custody of his teenage sons, says, "When my mother (72 years old and with severe vision difficulties) approaches me with the kind of attitude where she *asks* rather than *tells* me what I should do for her, we can work out just about anything. When she says, 'Greg, I know you're working two straight 12-hour shifts and I don't want to load you with extra chores, but I need groceries. Would it be possible for you to help out by picking up some things on your way home?' I'll always find a way." Respecting Greg's frenzied life and multi-family needs, she does not demand or dictate. Without violating boundaries, she compromises so each one's needs can be satisfied.

As parents ask not to be left out, children also ask for appropriate entre into their parents' lives. Respecting their boundaries for separation and autonomy, they ask parents to let them know when they are needed so they can be of support. They do not want to intrude, to over-protect to treat them like infants. They want to be there for parents on their terms.

Anne, a 52-year old bookkeeper whose 78-year-old mother, Mary, lives with her, is typical of this situation. Respecting Mary's need for control over her life (autonomy) and sensitive to her self-effacing personality, Anne said the following to her during a family session in my office:

> For God's sake, Mom, tell us when you're afraid to be alone. We can work things out so that when Tom and I go away for a weekend or vacation, you can be with someone. It's no trouble to do that with all the people in our family who love you and love to be with you. We know you bend over backward not to be a burden, but *we'll* tell you when you are. Give us a chance to be of help when we are able. This is our pleasure and privilege. We know you don't expect much and are always concerned about us. But you go too far sometimes! So just tell us what you want. We won't do more or less than you ask.

The relationship that Anne wants has room for the free expression of hurts, problems, and needs by *both* sides. It is the only relationship that makes sense between parents and children at this turning point because in its openess, it is the only one that can bring the closeness each desires. A relationship between adults who respect one another as equals, it also serves two important functions—it gives parents enough independence to maintain their autonomy, and it gives children the chance to live their own lives while becoming mature as sons and daughters.

On the surface, it would seem parents and children really want little from each other. Although parents certainly expect dependability, they do not want it at the expense of their children's well-being. Quite simply, they do not want to be a burden. And although children ask that parents only let them live their own lives, this in no way weakens their need for emotional attachment or filial maturity. Without question, grown children still seek their parents' love and affirmation, while also being more than willing to render necessary care. Even when parents have given little or been demanding, self-centered, or intimidating, children always manage to come through with whatever is needed at the final hour.

Almost paradoxically, however, the "little" each asks for is really a lot when looked at more closely. For at bottom of all the jockeying for a comfortable balance between attachment and separation and all the preaching about dependence and independence is the cry for emotional closeness. And "emotional closeness," "intimacy," or whatever you choose to call that special connection is not small stuff. Emotional closeness is when a mother knows her daughter will listen when she just needs to talk, when another parent knows that her son stops in every week for lunch because he wants to, or when others know their children's phone calls are motivated by genuine interest. Because interactions of this nature have the power to change a parent's mood from despair to happiness, they are hardly little nothings. They not only nourish and sustain us, they are the intimate connections that give life its fullest meaning.

In the same vein, when a mother understands that her daughter is too busy to visit every day but appreciates and acknowledges the things she *is* able to do for her, she spins a web of emotional closeness. By affirming that she is a "good" daughter, the mother also makes up for, even diminishes, any hurts from the past. Such validation is no small thing.

Likewise, when parents encourage their daughter and son-in-law to take a much-needed vacation, not only reassuring them they will be alright but reinforcing their children's need for recreation, they demonstrate the kind of respect of which emotional closeness is made. Seemingly inconsequential because it involves only a few words, it is a noble gesture unselfishly determined by their children's needs as adults instead of their power as parents.

The simple exchanges of warmth, kindness, and respect that create friendship between parents and children have a ripple effect. They are gifts that keep on giving. For example, parents who respect their children's needs and acknowledge the support they give them make their children even more lovingly dependable.

Be there for me when I need you yet respect me for who I am and how I live my life; give me space to be my own person and don't tell me what to do; speak to me frankly of our differences so we can compromise; show me you care by staying in touch and including me in family activities; share your feelings and thoughts;

tell me what it feels like to grow old—these are what parents and children seem to want from each other as they struggle to create intimacy during the precious, finite years of late life. Sounding more like peers than parent and child, they are appeals for friendship. Except for "Tell me what it's like to grow old," the requests tend to be interchangable between the generations, clearly indicating it is time for old boundaries to topple, giving way to less-rigid relationships between parents and children.

The term *intimacy at a distance*, coined by an Austrian gerontologist almost 40 years ago to describe the best connection for aged parents and their grown children, might be what this friendship is all about.[10] It refers to maintaining a distance between parents and children as a way for parents to sustain independence and to minimize conflict without destroying emotional closeness, and it has considerable merit.

However, much has changed since 1956 when this term was conceptualized. Since elders are living longer and children are becoming more involved in caring for them, the generations find themselves thrown together—for better or for worse. The number of programs and services designed to help the generations cope with this situation indicate that parents and children want it to be "for better." Children, at least, seem to want more meaningful involvement with their aging parents. The development of CAPS (Children of Aging Parents) groups, elder-care programs in the workplace, respite-care services, geriatric care managers, adult day-care centers, newsletters, and seminars for caregivers all attest to this trend.[11] "Intimacy at a distance," therefore, seems like an outdated way to describe what is happening between aging parents and their grown, caregiving children.

What I find astonishing is how much the pendulum has swung in just the last decade. In 1981, in his book *New Rules*, pollster Daniel Yankelovich, paints a picture of a cooler state of filial affairs:[12]

> One of the most far-reaching changes in norms relates to what parents believe they owe their children and what their children owe them. Nowhere are changes in the unwritten social contract more significant or agonizing. The overall pattern is clear: today's parents expect to make fewer sacrifices for their children than in the past, but they also demand less from their offspring in the form of future

obligations than their parents demanded of them. Measures of these attitudes in previous eras do not exist, largely because no one thought the parent-child bond as anything but permanent.

Breaking this down into measured categories, Yankelovich reported that 66 percent of American parents feel that they "should be free to live their own lives, even if it means spending less time with their children," and 67 percent believe that "children do not have an obligation to their parent regardless of what their parents have done for them."

Contrast these dire findings with a Gallup Poll (cited at the beginning of this chapter) done only eight years later and the clear impression is of a country whose values about family life have come almost full circle. What emerges from this research is a more optimistic picture about the future of the American family. In a poll for the *Los Angeles Times* Syndicate, Gallup interviewed 1,250 adults across the United States "to find out how far people live from their extended families, how often they visit and talk with their relatives, and how well they get along with different family members." The results show that: (1) Despite the mobility of the population, most adult children live fairly close to their parents. Two-thirds (67 percent) of adults with at least one living parent live within an hour's driving distance of a parent, including one in seven (13 percent) who lives in the same household as a parent. (2) People of all ages and circumstances look to their kinfolk as an important source of financial aid and help with day-to-day problems. But practical concerns are by no means the only reason Americans stay in touch with their relatives. *With few exceptions, people enjoy being with family members and wish they had more time to spend with them.*[13]

The more things change, the more some things stay the same. Despite social developments that tend to isolate us from those we love, aging parents and grown children not only remain emotionally committed but actually wish they had more time to spend with each other. If anything, the forces that are depersonalizing our modern era only heighten the importance of intimate human relationships.

How, then, do we best describe the reciprocal relationship needs of aging parents and grown children in today's world? If intimacy at a distance, though accurately reflecting parents' wishes to remain independent as long as possible, seems a bit cool, then what?

I believe "filial friendship" indicates what parents and children want from each other in their final years together. Because parents and children as kinfolk cannot be "just friends,"[14] *"filial friendship"* seems appropriate.

Friendship between parent and child? you might ask. Come on, even though both are older, is such a relationship even possible or right? After all, there are some things parents and children can't and shouldn't tell each other. Of course, there are. And there are some things *only* parents and children *can* tell each other. Whether they can or cannot reveal everything to each other does not matter. All friendships can tolerate just so much disclosure before bursting at the seams. The other criteria for friendship—acceptance, respect, affection, dependability, openness, and frankness—are all there. Precisely because both are older, it is the only relationship that makes sense. The out-dated parent-child connection only causes emotional distance, and closeness is the desired goal for both generations. What else is there?

Elsie, 72, a retired real estate broker, summed up the meaning of this friendship in these words:

> When my husband, Brad, required extensive surgery and radiation for a brain tumor and I couldn't bear to return alone to my home every night, I asked my son and daughter-in-law if I could temporarily move in with them until he was well. I felt I could never ask my friends for such a favor. But I knew I could with my children. Over the years we've become close and we know we can always count on each other. It just seemed so natural and right to ask them for their help. They know I'm not a busy-body—I don't ask a lot of questions or tell them what to do. I leave them alone, if you know what I mean. They can trust me not to take advantage of their love. How can I say it, there's just a feeling of trust there. We seem to understand and respect each other. I love people and have always been blessed with several very close friends, but for something like this I had to ask my children, who are also my friends, but in a different way. Do you know what I mean?

I do know. For me the meaning rings clear as a bell when, in initial counseling sessions, I ask my client to tell me something about the quality of his or her relationship to parents or children. When the response is "My children are my friends, of course," "We really like and respect each other," or "I'm lucky because I can usually talk to them about most anything," I always feel lighter. I am reassured my client does not stand alone; *family* is out there who will listen, understand, and provide support. Besides friendship, this person has that extra ingredient, that cushion of security, that human safety net only biological connection can provide. When our parents or our children can understand our hurt or happiness, it does make a difference. Their acceptance and approval are without equal.

Moreover, the fact that society generally accepts more relaxed interaction between parents and children is a healthy sign for filial friendship. Although the next chapter explores those changes in the family forms and norms that favor filial friendship, it is important to note that this is neither a toxic nor unnatural concept.

It is what forges the links of emotional closeness between generations. Also, as filial maturity is the final cycle of adulthood, filial friendship is the ultimate reward of raising children. To experience our grown children as friends is, in the final analysis, proof that as parents, we did a fairly good job. Whether or not filial friendship is owed, it is surely what most parents and children want.

And the Walls Come Down

"The rules keep changing" and "families aren't what they used to be" are the words of a song from the Broadway musical, *Falsettos*.[1] When I first saw them in an essay by Frank Rich, drama critic for the *New York Times*, I knew they would provide the perfect introduction to this chapter. They directly address the dramatic changes in families and family life occurring in America today.

The plot of *Falsettos*, which is about a husband who leaves his wife and son for a male lover, is not exactly mainstream Americana, but it is quintessentially contemporary. *Falsettos* acknowledges the demise of the nuclear family as the predominant family form. Now a minority within a larger, diverse framework of family structures, it is overshadowed by single-parent families, whether heterosexual or homosexual, and step-families.

As the increased rates of divorce, remarriage, and surrogate parenthood spawn these variations, they also give rise to the growth of three-generation families. Just as grown, never-married children return to their parents' homes to save money in an inflated economy, separated and divorced children also come home again. Needing either a place to live, help with baby sitting, or both, grown children with children often find themselves at their parents' doorsteps nowadays. According to a study published in 1986, quoted by Ken Dychtwald in his book *Age Wave*, "three out of ten grandparents said that the grandchild had come to live with them, often accompanied by the parent who had custody."[2]

When these children return home they are adults, but neverthe-less, they do return to their original nests. Whoever came up with the absurd notion that we can't go home again? Whoever said there comes a point when parents and children stop needing each other? Homecomings, whether short or long, occur throughout the life of the family for a variety of reasons and validate the concept of inter-dependence of the generations first mentioned in Chapter 2. They also reinforce the naturalness of parents and children asking things of one another and helping each other across the years.

The reverse phenomenon of elderly parents moving in with grown children, which Vivian Carlin and I wrote about in *Should Mom Live with Us*, is yet another variation of the interdependence theme.[3] Although such parents do not return "home" in a literal sense, reconnection with their children under the same roof to form a family unit is, nevertheless, a kind of symbolic coming home. Considering that today "for the first time in American histo-ry, the average married couple, by the time they are 40 years old, has more parents than children,"[4] it hardly comes as a surprise that some elderly parents find themselves at their children's front doors. The family of today, a far cry from the child-oriented family of pre-industrialized America, has different priorities and needs.

My favorite example of a multigenerational family with home-comings at both ends of the spectrum is the Jenning family. Origi-nally composed of Barbara, Kevin, and their three children, the family was a typical nuclear unit. Within a few years, however, the family was forced to extend itself to include two other generations. First, Barbara's 75-year-old widowed mother, Claire, moved in with them; three years later the Jenning's 20-year-old separated daughter, Maggie, returned home with her toddler son. If ever a couple felt "sandwiched" it was Barbara and Kevin. Buffeted by demands from four generations for space, privacy, and attention, there were days when the services of an expert mediator in domes-tic intergenerational relations would have been more than wel-come. Indeed, because the Jennings were willing to bump heads in family therapy sessions in my office, they succeeded in living together in friendship, based on mutual respect for everyone's needs.

The Jennings and other multigenerational homes are very much a phenomenon of the present. Back in those "good old days" parents usually did not live long enough to require long-term care. And back then the divorce rate was much lower.

If family forms have dramatically changed over the past 30 years, so has filial conduct within the family. There was a time when children called their fathers "sir" and the entire family had to be assembled at the dinner table. Back then, children were not allowed to speak unless spoken to and only certain harmless subjects could be addressed between parent and child. Parents and children never showed their real feelings. These norms, which resulted in fear rather than trust, secrecy rather than openess, and posturing rather than intimacy, have been generally replaced with more relaxed, egalitarian, and sensible ways of interacting.

What struck me most about Frank Rich's *New York Times* article was that he went to see and then reviewed *Falsettos* to educate his 8- and 12-year-old sons through the vehicle of theater about a different kind of family. The fact that he took them to see the show tells us more than his review does about the general loosening of the rules that once governed what parents and children said and did with each other. I can't imagine my father or any parent 40 or 50 years ago taking his or her kids to a play about a marital break-up because of same-sex infidelity. Never mind that plays on this subject did not exist back then. The point is that sex, in its many-faceted varieties, was a taboo area. Since it was unsuitable even as conversation between parents and children, it was highly unlikely to be an interest they would share through theater, film, or any other art medium.

Why explore sociological issues? What do they have to do with achieving friendship between grown children and their elderly parents?

The answers to these complex questions are simple enough. If people and social institutions are changing, as they have been in this country since the '60s and '70s, then the changes can be fairly widespread. Once barriers come tumbling down in one sector, their force may cause other, distant walls to topple. To illustrate, the civil rights movement of the 1960s that broke new ground for blacks also produced the fertile soil for a reexamination of issues between men and women. The latter development, a renewed interest in feminism, affected more than just the special interests of women. Its tremors shook other traditional beliefs, ultimately producing critical shifts in the ways people marry, parent, love, live, work, govern, and even dress. Our everyday, ordinary existence, including emotional life was touched by the changes when these destructive social barriers started to fall.

To be more specific, if there are many ways to be a family, then why shouldn't older people, like their younger counterparts, live according to their needs? If it's okay for young people to live together without being married, to live in communes or to have roommates, or to vacation in Club Med groups, why shouldn't old people have the same options? In fact elders are currently experimenting with different ways of living and travelling (Elderhostel, Travel Companion Exchange, *and* Club Med) to cope with the isolation and loneliness that often accompany the later years.[5] Or, if young people divorce and separate with relative ease, why can't old people do the same? They are—more people over age 50, no longer willing to remain in unhappy marriages, separate or divorce.[6] Or if racial and religious prejudice are intolerable, why not ageism? It is as groups such as the Gray Panthers, American Association of Retired Persons, the National Council of Senior Citizens, and the National Caucus on the Black Aged battle discrimination against people who are old. Or, if males and females are achieving equality in status and worth, why isn't the same kind of parity possible for grown children and their aging parents?

In other words, all things become possible in an atmosphere friendly to change. Two current trends provide a receptive climate for intergenerational friendship: less-stringent rules for filial behavior and new family structures—from single-parent and step-families to older three- and four-generation families where grandparents can play pivotal roles. As we all live longer, we become more alike in our adult needs for loving connection with friends and family.

The evolution of the American family in different directions is natural. Its new twists and turns do not signal social disaster; they represent social progress. For one thing, families do not stand still in a changing world. They must respond, moving along with major technological, economic, social, demographic, and cultural developments. The old rule that form follows function holds true for the family as well as for other areas such as work, recreation, education, and dress. The family that best suited the function of eighteenth century, agrarian United States would be an anachronism today. If they were to return and see working and commuting couples, day care for children, adult day care for older people, and men staying home to raise children while their wives work, they'd surely think they were on the wrong planet.

These once undreamed-of changes in family form have not lessened the need for the unique emotional closeness of families, however. No matter what form defines a particular family, members still crave attachment. Indeed, as Frank Rich poignantly writes in his review of *Falsettos*, ". . . the hero, Marvin, sings in his first number of his overwhelming desire to be part of 'a tightknit family, a group that harmonizes.' | "[7] Not at all different from the refrain parents and children chant to each other in later life (see the preceding chapter), it has relevance for families of all types, wherever they are in the life cycle.

As I look back to 1955 when my first child was born, when some would have us believe families were closer, I am struck by the absence of the ritual of bonding. If ever there was a symbol of the interdependence of the generations, it is "bonding." In 1955, however, the idea of my parents coming to the hospital to hold my son—to bond—during those first hours was, if not unheard of, absurd. Several years ago, however, when my first grandchild was born, my daughter insisted that my husband and I, and her father and his wife come to the hospital as quickly as possible. Not too long after Peter was handed to her, there we all were waiting for that ceremonial embrace. Of course, bonding is commonplace today, as hospitals even reserve special hours for the grandparents to bond with their new grandchildren.

As single-parent, step-parent, dual-career couple, and homosexual-parent families replace the rapidly disappearing nuclear family, something as seemingly ordinary as bonding reminds us that while some things change, others remain the same. What remains constant throughout the changing landscape of family relationships is the desire for warm, emotional attachments between the generations. The rite of bonding proves that children value connection with the older generation; that from day one they want their parents to be there to hold *their* children. It shows that they want them to be a living presence in their lives and to forge another link in the intergenerational chain.

The old order changes but what aging parents and middle-aged children want from each other does not. Emotional warmth and exchange, support, friendship, and being together in harmony remain. These basic human needs, however, cannot be met within a family where walls divide parents and children into the powerful and the powerless, the right and the wrong, infallible and the fallible.

Consider the following and their common theme:

New rules of filial etiquette for a new world
A *revised contract* for parents and children.
A *new way of operating* for both generations that allows them to relate as friends and peers
Role equality rather than role reversal
Filial liberation that is at the same time *parental liberation*

These statements speak of new forces that have changed the outdated rules we once lived by. They tell us to be unafraid of these positive and wholesome changes. Reaffirming the need for family connection, they also remind us that as parents and children age, the meaning of belonging to a caring group becomes more important. Both generations are bound by these warm human connections as well as by the need to be part of something larger than self. In other words, there comes a time when both generations are in the same boat.

Families may take many forms. People unite to suit their individual needs in a rapidly changing society. Regardless of the family's form, if they are able to talk, love, laugh, disagree, and cry without fear in an atmosphere of trust and respect, they are a family—and certainly a family of friends.

Ken Dychtwald in *Age Wave* speaks of "reinventing the family."[8] It is an apt term. However, whether we speak of reinvention, revision, new family rules, or filial or parental liberation, the message is clear: the old way no longer works for parents and children who will now spend many years together as adults.

It is very hard, for my generation's parents to accept the idea of a more egalitarian relationship with us. They were taught different rules, often determined by strong ethnic and cultural traditions, and the old ways die hard. When I listen to my father talk about what he sees and hears on the *Oprah Winfry* show, I appreciate how difficult it is for him to absorb the earth-shaking social changes he has witnessed in his lifetime. Riveted to the tv while shaking his head in shock and dismay, he groans, "My God, if my mother, but especially my father were alive to hear how plain parents and children talk to each other, they would think the world has gone crazy! They would faint dead in front of the tv set." Then switching to matters of mating and dating, he says with a sheepish grin, "I never looked a girl in the eyes until I came to this country. And now people talk on these shows about going to bed like it was nothing. They have no shame about telling everything they do. Maybe it's better this way, I don't know."

For my children and me, on the other hand, the shift to an equal, more open relationship seems almost natural. We have little, if any, difficulty living by these new rules. The division between us when they were young and dependent fell some 10 years ago when they were in their early twenties. Half by conscious choice, half by trial and error, I realized life would be less painful if I stopped dictating and lecturing to them about how they should live their lives. Accepting them as adults who have a right to do, to go, to love, to be and to believe as they choose, I not only have better times with them, but as equals we are emotionally closer. Without the self-imposed strain of having to be in tune with them all the time—worrying, rescuing, criticizing—I feel strangely liberated. Lighter, and with more time to invest in my own pursuits, I am off the parental hook at long last.

Of course, someplace deep inside me, I remain a parent. Despite other professional and personal achievements, being a parent is a core component of who I am. Worries over how my daughter will fare as a single mother, how one son will manage 3,000 miles away, and how another can live a sane life in New York City eternally plague me. Such thoughts, part and parcel of parenthood, are perfectly okay. For while I have given up the role of "parent" for the role of a friend, I will not give up these uniquely loving, yet uniquely ambivalent feelings.

Doris, a 50-year-old single mother I know who consciously, gave up the role of "parent," had these triumphant words to say about the entire experience.

> I decided when Frank (her son) turned 25 that I would make a new contract with him. He was working at a good job, had a girlfriend and friends, a life of his own, and I simply said to myself one

day, "It's time for us to stop being parent and child and to be friends."

I felt that our relationship would be closer and a lot more genuine if we could get rid of that parent-child barrier. I knew that sometimes I could come off as a know-it-all or opinionated and he would become angry and resent me. I wanted to represent something different in his life, not a parental authority figure. I guess I felt we could like each other a lot more if we dropped those old roles that make no sense today.

So one day I invited him for dinner to talk things over. I told him that we are both now adults and that I wanted us to be friends on this basis. I said to Frank, Let's from this time on only speak the truth to each other; no more you trying to please me because I'm your mother and me trying to be this perfect, all-knowing person who's always got things under control. Because I'm not. I worry, have doubts, make mistakes, have my insecurities just like you. So, let's be friends. Let's be real people with each other. It will be so much better this way, without pretense. I'm not saying we tell each other everything or that we run to each other with every problem. I don't want that and I know you don't either. But we must always tell each other how we feel when there is something bothering us that could keep us from being close. I don't want you to be afraid of telling me the truth about myself, like when I start to criticize you unfairly or when I start lecturing you on what *I* think is best for you or when I ask you too many nosy questions about your personal life. I always want us to be able to talk things out as people who understand and respect each other.

He thought what I had to say was just great. He told me I had a lot of courage to propose this and we would give it the best we could.

Well, it has been two years since that dinner where we sealed our friendship with a champagne toast. We are closer and more real to each than we've ever been. And although a year ago his job took him out west for an indefinite period of time, whenever we speak on the telephone all the love and respect we feel for each other comes right through. Sure I will always be his parent in the sense that he came from me and I raised him. But we are *friends*, and shouldn't this be the final goal of parenthood?

Doris and Frank are among the lucky few to recognize early on the benefits of changing the rules. Sarah and Lois (Chapter 4) reinvented their relationship later in life, but they are also fortunate that they *did* do it. It's never too late for parents and children to become friends. In fact, it's perhaps even sweeter when the remaining years are growing shorter. When both generations realize their mortality and the importance of loving connection in their lives, friendship assumes poignant proportions.

Worrying about the process and its eventual outcome become minor considerations compared to getting on with it—to just *doing* it. Molly (Chapter 5), whose fate was to "dance" alone, took a deep breath and confronted her mother once and for all. When Sarah, already in her '70s, finally decided to call her daughter Lois after years of blaming her for their estrangement, it was without second thought.

Never has there been a better time to destroy the hierarchical boundary between parent and child.[9] With social walls tumbling down everywhere, the notion of tearing down the wall dividing parents and their adult children seems hardly revolutionary. As a society top-heavy with adults, where "people regardless of their age, have more parents, grandparents, and great grandparents than has ever been true before,"[10] it stands to reason that we had better find more loving ways to relate to one another. It is both silly and painful to think about parents and children in the later years of their lives, relating to one another from their anachonristic roles.

The fact that people over 60 are entering psychotherapy in record numbers is a clear sign of both changing times and their desire to finish well with their children.[11] Courageously breaking from the stereotype that therapy is only for "crazy people" or those with serious problems, elders of this more private generation are taking the risk of stepping into a therapist's office. Many come for help with bereavement issues, but many others, like Sarah, come to resolve old conflicts with their children. Because time is running out, they frequently are able to do the work of therapy more quickly than their mid-life children. They get right to the point, honing in on the real issues distressing them. As I listen and respond, I think of a tree in winter. These elders are saying to me, Take me as I am. What you see is what there is. I've only time for the truth.

Some children, despite how hard they try, cannot convince their hard-hearted parents to bring down the walls. Their parents want to keep the barriers just as they are, either from fear of losing control or fear of taking a risk. In their despair, many children believe the wound caused by their parents' failure to see the light can never be healed.

I tell these children again and again to take heart. What you cannot accomplish with your parents, you can accomplish with your children. You must forgive your parents because they can only be what they are. But unlike them, you have learned life's lessons about growth and letting go. When you are old, which will be very soon, you will put these lessons to work with your children. As successful parents and grandparents, you will not only find recovery but savor the peace that eluded you for so long.

For adults without children, there also is hope. The wisdom gained from understanding our families is always valuable because it enables us to be whole individuals. Our capacity to be more loving, more accepting, and more emotionally generous is a force that enriches all our intimate relationships, not just with children. Certainly, children without children who have parents who do not respect them and who use control and intimidation appreciate the importance of kindness between all people.

The Last Dance

Using dance or dancing as a metaphor to describe significant relationships is common. It is frequently used by professionals concerned with interpersonal connections because it is such an elegant way to talk about basic human attachments. Psychologist Harriet G. Lerner titled three of her books *The Dance of Anger, The Dance of Intimacy*, and *The Dance of Deception*.[1] The spiritual teacher, Ram Dass, in writing about the "dance of life," calls his outstanding book *The Only Dance There Is*.[2]

The truth is that in life we generally do engage in one kind of dance or another with people to whom we are emotionally connected. Husbands and wives, brothers and sisters, friends and lovers all move with a variety of steps and tunes. Unlike the talented Rogers and Astaire, we are imperfect and clumsy, and have a much harder time. Stepping on each other's toes, misreading each other's cues, losing the rhythm, or even hearing different music, we more often than not find it difficult to stay in sync with our partners.

We might try to out-do a sibling we consider a rival rather than dancing harmoniously. Or if our partner is a spouse with whom we are angry, it might suit our vengeful side to sabotage the dance with a few deliberate false steps. Even when we're trying our best to be in step, we may unintentionally make mistakes.

The dance between parents and children is the most fascinating of all life's dances. The music and tempo change according to the phase and each party tries to adjust to the new rhythms. A marathon if ever there was one, it twists and turns over 60 or 70 years.³ The dance is full of a variety of toxic and wholesome entanglements, and it is ambivalent in nature because bonding by blood creates certain expectations and hopes. It remains fertile territory for exploration.

When the child is helpless and the parent capable and independent, a fluid synchrony seems to be at work. Parents sense their children's needs, while even the youngest, tiniest children can show their satisfaction by a contented smile or sigh. Parent and child are emotionally in tune with one another. The simple fact is that barring unforseen circumstances, this is how it is for most of us— smooth and easy. Vestiges of this relationship remain, but future dances will be less certain, less straightforward, and less smooth.

The tension between holding on and letting go, barely a factor in the almost-instinctive first dance, becomes more apparent in future dances. As children grow into adults and as parents relinquish their protective role, knowing what to say and when to say it or when to move in and when to pull back becomes less certain. By the time parents and children have their last dance, a simple offer of Why don't you let me wash those shirts for you or Perhaps you should think twice before spending so much money on a house might be distorted. With parents and children now stepping on each other's toes or tiptoeing fearfully, they actually are out of synch with each other.

The close physical and psychological connection necessary for the child's survival dissolves as children and parents grow older. Consequently, they must learn a new dance. The old relationship no longer will do, as children gradually pull away to make their own lives, as parents invest more time in outside interests and as the earlier, taut emotional wiring begins to fray.

As complicated as the years are in between, most people seem to manage them well. They learn as they go, clearly communicating their moves and intentions and, consequently, knowing when to let go and when to connect. Parents and children who are open to each other always seem to be there when necessary without dangerous strings of attachment. Though less primitive and less intense, the same responsiveness formed during the early years pervades their interactions: each asks only what the other can give, each appropriately recognizes the other's behavior, and each gives the other ample space for self-growth. When parents and children are able to do the work required for each stage of life, they develop step by step the wisdom necessary for harmony with each other in the later years. Of course, they make mistakes along the way— human relationships are always imperfect—but they learn from them and from each other the importance of flexibility, compromise, acceptance, and openness. They learn to let go of resentments, the necessity of being right all the time, and power as a way to get what they want.

Parents and children who for one reason or another bungled the earlier stages have a harder time moving into the last one. It's not that they don't want to move together in harmony and step; they simply do not know how. These are the parents and children I counsel and who seek me out after my talks, the people who tell me how painful it is to be disconnected from each other at this time of their lives. If they do not understand the choreography of the last dance, it is because they never learned the earlier steps. At times things may have gone well enough to learn some basic moves, but somewhere along the way, the emotional pain, the misunderstanding, and the resentment got in the way of their learning.

The last dance is unique because it signals the end, which means there is no more time to make it right, do it differently or better. The nearness of death coupled with a yearning for connection forces parents and children to do now what they could not do before—come together as equal for the affection and closeness that is unique to their bond.

Parents who were written off as not likely to change often surprise us with their eagerness to learn a few new ideas. Challenging the absurd assumption that old people are unable to grow and learn, they do whatever is necessary to achieve a warm connection with their children. They stop squandering precious time in old resentments and ancient battles for control because they are determined to be remembered as loving parents and people. They soften where they were once hard, listen where they once only wanted to be heard, and give where they once could only withhold.

Their children, frustrated from years of trying and missing closeness, are also ready to do things differently. Middle-aged and feeling the clutch of fleeting time as deeply as their parents, they are willing to approach them as equal adults. Their adolescent anger is replaced with sincere determination to understand their parents as people and to let go of old hurts. The tone that predominates is sadness over the time that was wasted in pointless opposition. As they struggle to achieve wholesome relationships with their own children, they realize the best place to begin is with their own parents. They want to make one final stab at getting things right with their parents, hoping the pieces will fall into place when they become old and must depend on their own children for loving support.

The last dance is a mutual acknowledgment of love by people who now understand what life is about, allowing for the mature expression of feelings and thoughts. Parents and children can tell each other what they mean to each other, what they like and dislike about each other, and what memories they cherish.

The essence of the last dance is truth that springs from compassion and is meant to heal. Parents and children remove old masks, recognize one another's vulnerabilities, and finally express their pleasure in one another.

Although parents at this stage are usually dependent upon their children, roles do not reverse so that children become their parents' parents. Parents remain parents, but now they can trust their children's dependability.

It is a time for parents to let children help. Children, in turn, must respect their parents' choices about how to live their lives. They must forgive each other for only doing the best they could. And, of course, it is the time for parents to become mentors and sages to their children—to teach them about growing old and dying drawing on their own experience for life's final lessons.

For parents and children whose late-life relationships with each other have been more struggle than joy and who have almost given up hope, the opportunities for a new start are always there. Parents and children must be alert to their signals because they crop up when least expected. The following four vignettes illustrate the chancy nature of last opportunities and, as a result, the importance of seizing them when they occur.

Louise grudgingly flies out to California to care for her widowed, 81-year-old father, Paul, whom she never liked. Louise doesn't have to go. She has enough money to hire a geriatric-care manager to coordinate services for him. But she feels she must, because it would be the right thing to do. After being at his side constantly for almost a month, helping him to bathe and dress, and eating three meals a day with him, she not only comes to understand him for the person he is, but actually finds out she likes him. Those weeks, while brief, bring them a closeness they had never known. Sharing thoughts and feelings, reminiscing about a mutual past, pouring through old photograph albums, feeling free to express anger long suppressed, laughing and crying together, and finally forgiving each other, they relate as equal human beings who happen to be father and daughter. When Louise least expects it, when she believes her reservoir of hope had dried up, she and her father are given a last chance.

For Dorothy, 79, self-centered and demanding, the last dance begins when she tells her 50-year-old daughter, Robin, with whom she lives, how sorry she is for all the time she missed being with her when she was a child. Traveling with her busy and prominent husband instead of spending those precious years with Robin, Dorothy apologizes for being a neglectful mother. Now reigning from a wheelchair and still imperious, Dorothy is surprisingly responsive to her daughter's exasperation and resentment. She tells Robin she knows she failed as a mother; that, in fact, she never really understood what mothering was all about anyway. She says that half the time she never knew what to do with either Robin or her brother and that she relied upon the housekeeper so much because she felt so inept and helpless as a parent, not because she didn't love her children. She prays Robin will forgive her. With courageous honesty, she tells Robin, "In many ways, I was a child while I was raising you and probably still am."

As Robin relates her mother's words, she begins to sob, "And do you know what? My mother actually thanked me for taking her into my home and told me I was the good daughter she probably doesn't deserve to have." And so, Dorothy held out her hand to Robin to begin their final dance together.

For George, the last dance begins in the eleventh hour as his father, Phillip, is dying. After years of emotional exile from his father enforced by his possessive, autocratic mother, who was jealous of any time George and his father spent together, George finally reconnects with Phillip. George's rescuer, a seasoned hospice nurse sensitive to his and his father's wishes, entreats his mother to let them have time alone together. Despite initial protests, his mother steps aside and father and son come together. During the two months before Phillip' death, he and George, make up for a missed lifetime.

Muriel and her mother, Irene, experience renewal in the nursing home where Irene lives. Never having had a meaningful conversation with each other, sadly, they continue their superficial interactions during Irene's biweekly visits. One afternoon, Irene, now in a wheelchair and seemingly drained of spirit, grabs Muriel's hand. She procedes to tell Muriel with uncharacteristic animation about her unhappy marriage to her father, her many regrets over all she did not do with her life, and her sadness that she and Muriel are not closer. Although she knows she has little time, she hopes they might be able to talk openly, so Muriel's memories of her will be of their hours spent now instead of all the "nothing" that went before.

When Sarah, whom we met in Chapter 4, phones her daughter, Lois, their relationship begins to change. When Jane of Chapter 5 takes her mother to the theater, they start a fresh new phase. It doesn't matter whether it is parent or child who reaches out first. What matters is that the emotional silence is broken and that someone has the courage to speak the words of connection.

Even if the dance is brief, it is of value. George and his father, Phillip, had only two months together, Muriel and Irene, almost three years. For Sarah, now in her 80s, and her daughter, Lois, it continues. The length of the dance is unimportant. Only its quality counts.

However the last dance starts, whatever its path and longevity, it is good. Coming together in love and forgiveness can only be healing. The bumpy road that is the path for some children and their parents does not detract from its worth. It may well be that for those who have to work harder for reconciliation and have less time, it is even sweeter.

Remember that the last dance cannot happen without two willing, mature, and motivated partners. Once I gave more weight to the perspective of children, since the major part of my clinical work is with middle-aged people. I have grown to appreciate the plight of their parents, however. Since writing my first book, I have dealt with enough parents to be more in touch with the bitter pain they experience when long-held expectations are not fulfilled. Surprisingly, my deeper empathy is for them instead of their children. Their hurt can be especially intense during these final years because unlike their children, whose lives bubble with relationships and happenings, theirs may be a lonely existence. Deprived of the comraderie of friends who have died or are too disabled to socialize, they often live alone, isolated from the warmth and stimulation of relationships. The sad fact is often their children are the only people they have to depend on for care, support, and company. Not knowing how to handle the disappointment they feel, they push their children further away with harsh criticism, moral orders, and reprimands. Conditioned by old rules of behavior, they unwittingly create the opposite of what they truly desire. They want to dance but make all the wrong moves.

I want to help elderly parents understand enough about their children's struggles to appreciate the wisdom of approaching them with a lighter hand. Although some parents may feel that I am asking them to surrender the control and power inherent in parenting, the gain is greater than the loss. In blessing their children for what they can give instead of damning them for what they cannot, and in respecting them for who they are instead of faulting them for what they could not be, they win their children's love and devotion.

I want to reassure parents that their children care about them and are committed to caring for them. Knowing their children do honor them, although differently than they had expected, might ease their feelings of abandonment and loneliness. It is a big leap of faith for parents to trust in this new "honor." But too much is at stake for them to turn their backs on this final opportunity for connection. There will not be another chance.

Despite my sympathy for parents, like Dr. Harry Berman, I believe that in the final analysis they hold the trump card.[4] By withholding filial maturity from their children by not allowing them to be dependable adults, they guarantee that their last chance to reunite will fail. Theirs is a shallow victory. I can only say to them that sometimes in order to have control it must be given up. Although in old age control can easily take on the guise of life itself, it is life's antithesis. Living life richly and fully in all its splendid moments requires, not tightly holding on, but letting go—trusting and opening up to life's surprises. You need your children for the endearing connection only they can give; stubborn, self-righteous posturing only creates distance.

Parents need to know certain things. First of all, that their children are committed to their welfare and want to hear about what it is like in the winter of life, but they cannot live their old age for them. They need to understand that social and cultural changes strain old rules of filial etiquette and they need to know how hard they make it for themselves by adhering to obsolete, authoritarian parental roles. Parents must also understand that relying on strangers for help does not betray family values; in fact, it frees their children to be with them in more meaningful ways. Although their children cannot take the place of friends who have died, they can be there for them with emotional sustenance. Their children, though grown up, still want to come home again for that special, unconditional acceptance only parents have the power to give.

Children need to know that their parents' genuine fears of abandonment may distort well-meaning expressions for support into pernicious demands and manipulation. Although they cannot live their parents' old age, they must at least sympathize with the sad losses it spawns and meet their parents as the adults they are. They should understand that at this stage of life, being afraid of their parents is totally inappropriate. It is important to forgive their parents' mistakes and realize they did the best they could. Children should recognize that their aging parents cannot be the towers of strength they once were. Giving up this longing for eternally strong parents is painful; not only does it hurt to watch them fade but it makes us realize that soon we will too. Children also need to know it is okay to grieve for the loss of their parents as they once were and for the ultimate loss of their own selves, and that if their parents won't dance with them, they can still one day dance with *their* children.

What both generations must remember above all else, is that essentially they yearn for the same thing—warm, affectionate connection with each other. Despite unresolved conflicts from the past, they can learn to dance with each other in this final hour, if they are willing.

What both generations need to be reminded of over and over again is the disturbing notion that somehow it is the duty of children to provide total care to their parents. (See Chapters 3 and 4.)

Churning out shame and guilt in children and hostility and bitterness in parents, it is one of the major stumbling blocks preventing them from achieving the warm exchange they desire. To both generations, I say, "Give it up, once and for all! Parents, you will not get total return from your children. Children, you will not get it from your own children when your time comes." The score cannot be evened. The only way children can return the gift is to be the best parents they can to their own children.

As long as we choose connection and its loss nags like the phantom pain of a missing limb, we will keep trying to get things right with each other. The embers of forgiveness always burn.

For some parents and children, however, dancing together is simply out of the question. These parents are too frightened because of their own wounds to give up the high ground or too self-centered to make room for their children's needs. Generally, they are the "difficult" parents I mentioned in Chapter 2 and about whom I wrote in detail in *Your Best Is Good Enough*.[5] Insensitive to their children's needs, unable to acknowledge that their children have lives that do not include them, and disappointed at every turn with their children's caregiving efforts, they systematically destroy all chances for intimacy. Not only are they unable to dance, but their children do not wish to dance with them.

Children without the gift of care or who have been abused also do not wish to dance with their parents—and rightfully.[6] They cannot be held at fault for wanting distance from them.

If we won't grow up, wishing to remain forever helpless children who deny their elderly parents' waning strength (like Roseanne of Chapter 3) we are also unable to take part in the last dance. We must acknowledge our parents' old age with a commitment to be dependable.

The last dance is a meaningful way to say thank you for the gift of the first dance of life because it lets children return to parents *appropriately* some of the wonderful things they did for them. It also offers a way to thank children for the gifts of being exactly who and what they are and for being there for them as adults who hold out a dependable hand. It represents the completion of the final task of parents: to draw on their own experiences—their wisdom—to teach their children about the road of old age.

For both generations, there is the gratification of knowing that the trials, tribulations, fear, and pain of their long, complex connection were worth what they now enjoy; that all the dark tunnels they traveled together led to light.

We have the opportunity to pay final respect to each other, not at the gravestone or as a psychotherapeutic exercise, but while we are both alive—to hear it, feel it, experience it, acknowledge it, and, ultimately, rejoice in it. In the words of Dr. Abraham Heschel from his speech to the White House Conference on Aging on January 9, 1961, "The real bond between two generations is the insights they share, the appreciation they have in common, the moments of inner experience in which they meet."[7]

Notes

Introduction

1. Vivian E. Greenberg, *Your Best Is Good Enough: Aging Parents and Your Emotions* (New York: Lexington Books, an imprint of Macmillan, 1989).
2. Neil Simon, *Lost in Yonkers* (New York: Random House, 1991).
3. Greenberg, 30.
4. Daniel Goleman, "Erikson, in His Old Age, Expands His View of Life," *New York Times*, 14 June 1988, sec. C.
5. Elaine Brody, *Women in the Middle* (New York: Springer, 1990), 27.

Chapter 1. Why at Fifty Plus?

1. Melinda Beck, "Finding Work after Fifty," *Newsweek*, 16 March 1992, 58.
2. Robert Anderson, "I Never Sang for My Father," in *The Best Plays of 1967–68* (New York: Dodd, Mead, and Company), 281.
3. Lee Headley, *Adults and Their Families in Family Therapy* (New York: Plenum Press, 1977).
4. Margaret Blenkner, "Social Work and Family Relationships in Later Life with Some Thoughts on Filial Maturity," in *Social Structure and the Family: Generational Relations* (Englewood Cliffs, N.J.: Prentice-Hall, Inc., 1965), 46–59. A fuller explanation of the concept of filial maturity will be presented in Chapter 5.
5. Elaine M. Brody, "Parent-Care as a Normative Stress" (Paper presented at annual conference, Marriage Council of Philadelphia, Division of Family Studies, University of Pennsylvania, November, 1984.)
6. Ken Dychtwald, *Age Wave* (New York: Bantam Books, 1990), 252.
7. Scott Spencer, "The Old Man and the Novel," *New York Times*, 22 September 1991, sec. 6.
8. Rabbi Cary Kozberg, review of "Your Best Is Good Enough," by Vivian E. Greenberg, *The Ohio Jewish Chronicle* (October 3, 1991), 3.
9. CAPS (Children of Aging Parents) provides information and referral services for caregivers throughout the country. Among its many valuable services are a 24-hour answering service, a newsletter called the *Capsule*, and assistance in the development of support groups throughout the country. To receive infor-

mation about the organization, send a self-addressed, stamped envelope to the CAPS office: CAPS, 1609 Woodbourne Road, 302A, Levitown, PA 19057, phone 215-945-6900.

Anecdotal material in the form of inspiring personal essays collated by Phillip Berman are noteworthy: *The Courage to Grow Old*, Ballantine Books, New York, 1989, and *The Ageless Spirit*, also Ballantine Books, 1992.

Phillip Roth's *Patrimony*, Simon and Schuster, New York, 1991, and Tom Koch's *Mirrored Lives*, Praeger, New York, 1990, each about caregiving sons, are worthy of mention. One of the earliest and still most outstanding literary works about caregiving is, of course, Madeleine L'Engle's *The Summer of the Great-Grandmother*, Farrar, Straus & Giroux, New York, 1974. F. Forrester Church's biography of his father, U.S. Sen. Frank Church, *Father and Son*, Faber and Faber, 1985, is also highly recommended. The chapters devoted to the illness and death of the author's father are particularly relevant.

Self-help books for caregivers are generally increasing, with specialized magazines such as *Answers* (The Magazine Devoted to the Children of Aging Parents) 5725, Paradies Drive, Suite 400, Corte Madera, CA, 94925, and *Parent Care*, (Newsletter for Children of Aging Parents) Box 216, Bethany, OK, 73008, beginning to appear on the market.

Chapter 2. What's Growing Up All About?

1. Ayn Rand, *The Fountainhead* (New York: New American Library, 1952).
2. An explanation of separation-individuation can be found in one of the many writings on the subject by Dr. Margaret S. Mahler: "On the First Three Subphases of the Separation-Individuation Process," *International Journal of Psycho-Analysis* 53, (1972), 333–38.
3. James Framo, *Explorations in Marital and Family Therapy* (New York: Springer Publishing Co., 1982), 188.
4. Pat Conroy, *The Prince of Tides* (New York: Bantam Books, 1991), 8.
5. Robert Frost, *You Come Too*. (New York: Holt, Rinehart and Winston, 1965), 69–75.
6. Gloria Steinem, *Revolution from Within* (Boston: Little, Brown, 1992).
7. Virginia Satir, *The New Peoplemaking* (Mountainview, Calif.: Science and Behavior Books, Inc., 1988), 33.
8. Ibid., 33.
9. Greenberg, 128.
10. M. Scott Peck, *The Road Less Traveled* (New York: A Touchstone Book, Simon and Schuster, 1978), 71–72.

Chapter 3. I Won't Grow Up!

1. Henry T. Close, "On Parenting," *Voices*, Spring, 1968, 94.
2. Framo, 190.

3. Gina Kolata, "New Views on Life Spans Alter Forecasts on Elderly," *New York Times*, 16 November 1991.
4. *Vocal Selections from Peter Pan*, Edward H. Morris & Company, a Division of MPL Communications, Inc. 1954, 22.
5. Elaine M. Brody, quoted in column by Richard Louv, *San Diego Union*, 29 September 1991, 2.
6. Vivian F. Carlin and Vivian E. Greenberg, *Should Mom Live with Us: And Is Happiness Possible if She Does?*, (New York: Lexington Books, an imprint of Macmillan, 1992).
7. Alice Miller, *The Drama of the Gifted Child* (New York: Basic Books, 1990), 14.
8. Salvador Minuchin, *Families and Family Therapy* (Cambridge: Harvard University, 1979), 97.

Chapter 4. A Parent for All Seasons

1. Jonathan L. York and Robert J. Caslyn, "Family Involvement in Nursing Homes," *The Gerontologist*, 1977, vol. 17, 500–505.
2. Cheryl Simon, "The Myth of Abandonment," *Psychology Today*, April, 1988, 47.
3. Ethel Shanas, The Robert W. Kleemier Award Lecture, "Social Myth as Hypothesis: The Case of the Family Relations of Old People," *The Gerontologist*, vol. 19, no. 1, 1979.
4. Cheryl Simon, Myth of Abandonment. ???47
5. Harry J. Berman, "Adult Children and Their Parents: Irredeemable Obligation and Irreplaceable Loss," *Journal of Gerontological Social Work* vol. 10, 1.2, January, 1987, 33. This quote is used again in Chapter 5. ("Dancing Solo") where the concept of "filial maturity" is spelled out.
6. Headley, 186.
7. Erik Erikson, Joan Erikson, and Helen Kivnick, *Vital Involvement in Old Age* (New York: W.W. Norton, 1986), 75.
8. Emily Hancock, *The Girl Within* (New York: Fawcett Columbine, 1989), 182–206.
9. When a parent is dead, there are other ways to work through old issues. Writing letters, or the Gestalt technique of talking to an empty chair that stands in for the parent, are both effective in helping children express all they wished to say to their parents but never did. In this way feelings of anger, guilt, resentment, and sadness may be brought to completion.
10. Hancock, 204–206.
11. Erikson, 74.
12. Ibid., 327.
13. Thomas R. Cole, *The Journey of Life* (New York: Cambridge, 1992), 227–251.
14. Else Frenkel-Brunswik, "Adjustments and Reorientation in the Course of the

Life Span," *Middle Age and Aging* (Chicago: The University of Chicago Press, 1975), 84. In addition to this reference, Dr. Peck's article, referred to in footnote 8 of Chapter 6 is also useful in spelling out the tasks of middle and old age. The emphasis in both articles is on the necessity for middle-agers and old-agers to emotionally disengage from interests and activities of a physical nature. By middle age, a switch is required, whereby individuals begin to value wisdom and human relationships over physical strength, athletic prowess, and physical attractiveness. Identity now rests upon the development of these areas.

15. Frenkel-Brunswick, 84.
16. David Gutman, "Aging Among the Highland Maya: A Coposite Study," *Middle Age and Aging* (Chicago: The University of Chicago Press, 1975), 444–52. Dr. Gutman studied 40 Highland Mayan men in Mexico between the ages of 30 and 90 and found similarities in adaptive processes with their urban American male counterparts. This major developmental task consists of a shift in emotional investment from action, achievment, and competition to wisdom, thought, and the company of friends.
17. Ken Dychtwald, *Age Wave* (New York: Bantam Books 1990), 342–51. These pages provide a more in-depth discussion of the concept of "the third age." Of note, too, is the establishment of The Third Age Center at Fordham University in New York City. Founded by Monsignor Charles Fahey, it is a department of study devoted to human development in later life.
18. Abraham J. Heschel, "To Grow In Wisdom," from a speech to the 1961 White House Conference on Aging, Washington, D.C., 22.
19. Peck, p. 150.
20. Gay Gaer Luce, *Your Second Life* (New York: Delacorte Press/Seymour Lawrence, 1979).
21. Paul Arthur Schilpp, in *The Courage to Grow Old*, (New York: Ballantine, 1989) 313–314.
22. Patricia Leigh Brown, "When the Need to Help Won't Take Early Retirement," *New York Times*, 29 November 1990, sec. C. The article notes that the number of people taking early retirement is rising and their median educational level is going up—to 12.1 years in 1988, compared to 8.7 years in 1970. In 1989, people reaching age 65 could expect to live an average of 17 years longer.
23. Ibid, 12.
24. Ibid, 1.
25. *As You Like It*, act 2, sc. 7.

Chapter 5. Dancing Solo

1. Berman, 33.
2. Lillian Troll, "The Family of Later Life: A Decade Review," *Journal of Marriage and the Family*, May, 1971, 277.

3. Margaret Blenkner, 46–59.
4. Ibid., 46–59.
5. Framo, 188.
6. Blenkner, 46–59.
7. Close, 94.
8. Donald S. Williamson, "Personal Authority Via Termination of the Intergenerational Hierarchical Boundary: A 'New' Stage in the Family Cycle," *Journal of Marital and Family Therapy*, October, 1981, 447. This article forms the basis of my thoughts about the roles of parents and children in the second half of life.
9. Ibid.,

Chapter 6. What Do We Owe?

1. Larry Hugick, "Women Play the Leading Role in Keeping Modern Families Close," *The Gallup Poll News Service*, vol. 54, no. 9, 3 July 1989.
2. Barbara S. Vanderkolk and Ardis A. Young, *The Work And Family Revolution* (New York: Facts on File, 1991), 4–9.
3. Ibid., 104.
4. Blenkner, 46–49.
5. Kahlil Gibran, *The Prophet*, (New York: Alfred A. Knopf, 1964), 18–19.
6. Greenberg, 18.
7. David McCullough, *Truman* (New York: Simon and Schuster, 1992), 572.
8. Dr. Robert Peck, in his seminal article, "Psychololgical Developments in the Second Half of Life," clearly describes the tasks of middle age and old age. He finds that middle-agers, like old-agers, understand the importance of shifting emotional energy away from physical interests. "Valuing wisdom over physical powers and socializing over sexualizing," the middle-aged and elderly appreciate the importance of connection and closeness to others. Dr. Peck's article appears in *Psychological Aspects of Aging*, American Psychological Association, Washington, D.C., 1955, 44–48.
9. Hancock, 234.
10. Leopold Rosenmayr, "The Family—A Source of Hope for the Elderly," *Family, Bureaucracy and the Elderly* (Durham, N.C.: Duke University Press, 1977), 139.
11. See footnote 9, Chapter 1 and footnote 2, Chapter 7, on the expanded role of grandparents as indicative of the increasing importance of intergenerational connection in our society.

Private geriatric-care management is also a new service for caregivers. Managers, including social workers, nurses, psyhchologists, and gerontologists, provide consultation, counseling, placement, crisis intervention, and advocacy. They may assess, coordinate and monitor services to the elderly and their families or supply them directly. Their services are of special value to children who live at a distance from their elderly parents, since they provide up-to-date reports on their parents' status. To find care managers in your area, write to the National Association of Private Geriatric Care Managers, 655 North Alvernon Way, Suite 108, Tuscon, Arizona 85711.

12. Daniel Yankelovich, *New Rules* (New York: Random House, 1981), 103–104.
13. Hugick, 1.
14. Lillian Rubin, *Just Friends* (New York: Harper & Row, 1986). The notion of "just friends" is derived from the title of Rubin's book. A scholarly, yet moving treatise on the differences between kinship and friendship, it is well worth reading.

Chapter 7. And the Walls Come Down

1. Frank Rich, "Discovering Family Values at 'Falsettos," *New York Times*, 12 July 1992.
2. Dychtwald. The increased role of grandparents today deserves special mention. Not only does Dychtwald discuss this at length, but Sage Publications, Inc., of Newbury Park, California has published a series of books designed to help grandparents achieve more rewarding relationships within their families. Some of the titles in this series are: *Achieving Grandparent Potential, Grandparent Education*, and *Becoming A Better Grandparent*.
3. Carlin and Greenberg,
4. Cheryl Simon, quoting sociologist Samuel H. Preston, "The Myth of Abandonment," *Psychology Today*, April, 1988, 47.
5. R. Butler and M. Lewis, *Love and Sex After 60* (New York: Harper and Row, 1988), 121.
6. Dychtwald, 218.
7. Rich.
8. Dychtwald, 233.
9. Williamson, 447.
10. Elaine Brody, "Women in the Middle and Family Help to Older People," *The Gerontologist*, vol. 21, no. 5, 1981, 473.
11. Leslie Dreyfous, "Over-60 Set Happy with Therapy," *Palm Beach Post*, 3 January 1993, 1F.

Chapter 8. The Last Dance

1. Harriet G. Lerner, *The Dance of Anger* (New York: Harper & Row, 1985); *The Dance of Intimacy* (New York: Harper & Row, 1990); *The Dance of Deception* (New York: Harper Collins, 1993)
2. Ram Dass, *The Only Dance There Is* (New York: Anchor Books/Doubleday, 1974).
3. James Bennet, "When Elderly Care for Their Elders, *The New York Times*, October 4, 1992.
4. Berman, 21–33.
5. Greenberg, 127–133.

6. "Children Without the Gift of Caring" is the title of Chapter 9 of my book. The title was inspired by an article written by Elaine Brody entitled "All Generations Need the Gift of Caring," appearing in the *National Association of Social Workers News*, March, 1986, 9.

"Some children are unable to give care to their parents because they themselves have not received the 'gift of caring' from their parents. The degree to which all of us can give care and love depends to a large extent on what we were given by our parents somewhere along the line." (Excerpted from *Your Best Is Good Enough*.)

7. Abraham Heschel, 22.

Index